ISBN13: 978-1-959350-12-5

Set in: Georgia 10/11/12pt, Symbola 10pt

The Three Little Sisters
USA/CANADA

©The Three Little Sisters

-Footnotes have been converted to endnotes-

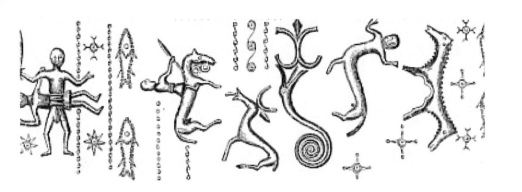

THE POETIC EDDA

SIX COSMOLOGY POEMS

TRANSLATED, INTERPRETED AND COMMENTED ON BY MARIA KVILHAUG

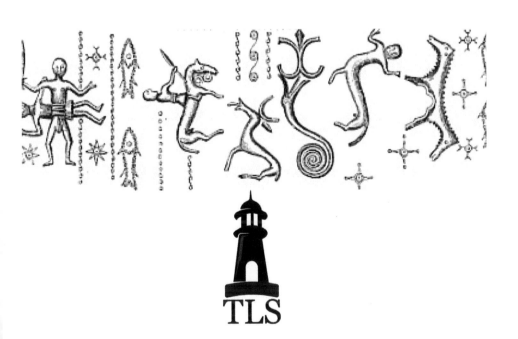

TLS

DEDICATION

I dedicate this book with translations and interpretations with explanations of six Edda poems about cosmology to my readers, viewers and followers who have encouraged me to continue my work on sharing my research on Old Norse myths.

Contents

ABOUT THE TRANSLATION

TRANSLATING NORSE MYTHOLOGY

"I wrote this book so that young students of poetry could learn to decipher that which has been composed in subtle manner." Snorri Sturluson: Introduction to the Prose Edda

When I started to seriously study Old Norse myths, I began reading the Poetic Edda in various translations from the Old Norse and mainly into Norwegian (my native language) and English (my second language). I realized that all the translations differed from each other, sometimes considerably so, and that the translation of poetry into another language – especially when the original language belongs to another age and a different, more archaic mentality – is always a matter of interpretation. However, to treat the myths like riddles that have to be interpreted and solved was in fact at the heart and core of Old Norse poetry, and is much of the reason why they are so interesting.

Old Norse myths were rendered in an allusive language of poetry that was profoundly metaphorical, symbolical and allegorical. A profound understanding of Viking Age Norse Heathenism is necessary to truly grasp the language in which the myths were spoken, as well as a basic understanding of the language itself. It is a grave mistake to try to read the myths literally as if they were stories of actual, supernatural "people". That kind of approach may lead to condescending conclusions: Either that the stories are fairy tales that superstitious and simple-minded idolatrous Heathen barbarians literally believed in, or that they were meant for the entertainment of children.

Some modern Heathens may also fail to see the deeper meanings conveyed by the ancestors if they try to take the myths as literal stories of divine human-like beings. It is important to bear in mind that Old Norse poets were not just reciting ancient ritual incantations: They were creative poets who composed poetry of their own. The Edda poems contain a lot of ancient themes and profoundly Heathen material, but they have also been composed by poets who had an agenda: To convey wisdom through the art of metaphors. The scalds, as they were called, worked quite freely, like modern poets, with the mythologies of their culture.

Gods and other supernatural entities that held a life of their own within the Heathen religion, beings revered, feared, invoked and worshiped in various ways – are, in Old Norse poetry, to a great degree taken out of their religious context in order to serve as literary characters. The ancient and (to the Heathens) well- known entities and their many names were employed in poetry to fulfill a function as metaphor and symbol of the many different powers that rule our lives from within the human mind and from the greater cosmos. Óðinn and Þórr, for example, were ancient gods in their own rights, but in the myths they are used to play out a particular literary and poetical function: They have become metaphors. This is why gods that we know were widely respected and revered could in fact be the objects of fun in the myths, such as the god Þórr ["Thór"], whose religious status as a god of thunder, marriage, protection and the enforcement of law and order has become less important in the myths about him than his literary role as a metaphor – or a symbol - of the human mind.

The poets could not have treated their gods with such license had it not been a recognized method of creating the poetry and meaningful tales that we know as "myths". Real Heathen gods and goddesses with cults and priesthoods of their own were employed in poetry right next to other beings that appear to have had no place within the religious cults whatsoever, but are still extremely important in the mythical lore. A well-known example of this is Loki, a god in the Edda mythology and yet one of which there is no trace in place-names or any other indication that he was ever worshiped by anyone.

Yet, he plays an important role in the myths, mainly because he has a literary function: A Viking Age scald, Thióðolf of Hvínir, who lived during the late 9th century, called Loki, among many other things, "The Mover of the Stories" [Sagna Hrærir]. The reason being that Loki's most important literary function was to be the accelerator of conflict, friction and thus movement and drama in the mythical stories. Thus he appears more frequently in Viking Age poetry than most deities that were actually worshiped. Baldr is another such poetical invention, representing the wisdom and courage that stems from a broad mind willing to see the entire picture, which leads to justice and the lack of judgment upon others. His death is the "death" of this quality in the world or within the individual, and his "killer" is another poetical invention whose name says all: Strife the Blind [Höðr Blindi].

Baldr´s "avenger", who puts Strife the Blind on the pyre, is simply called "The Choice" [Váli]. As soon as the choice is born, he takes action. This is not a way of saying that the son of a god can act as a warrior from the day he is born, but a way of saying that when the choice is truly made to put an end to blind, ignorant strife, it will begin to work. By taking the names and the functions of characters seriously, it becomes plain to see that the entire story is a parable of how ignorant aggression will bring wisdom and true observation six feet under, and that one has to consciously choose to get rid of this obstacle. It is an allegory, employing well-known literary characters that are said to be related to the gods, yet were never truly the objects of any known cult with the real-life Heathen religion.

The Edda myths are literature, fiction if you will, but made, I am sure, by Heathens with a profound understanding of the wisdom traditions that existed within the Heathen world. The primary function of the Norse myths that we are left with is in my opinion to convey a meaningful message: One that usually had to do with existential questions, metaphysical speculations, spiritual teachings or divination. Often they evidently reflect Heathen cult, ritual and religion, but even so the sacred powers are employed as means of creating literature. The mythical beings of the Norse traditions function, in the myths we have left to us, as symbols of literature, representing not so much actual divine or supernatural "persons" as they represent aspects of cosmos or of human experience.

Singular characters representing such basic aspects were revealed in many different forms, disguised behind many different kinds of names that all describe the particular role of the character in one particular setting. Old Norse myths work as parables, as ways of saying one single thing in countless different ways. Within this context, even the most sacred of entities could be treated with poetical license. The translator often has to choose between a literal translation and a paraphrased adaption that will make the text understandable in a modern language and a modern conception. Often, literal translations will make little or no sense to the modern reader, not only because the ancient language is so different, but because the minds behind the ancient language belong to a culture so different from ours. We simply do not possess the same concepts, and even if we try to approach and understand their concepts, it will be as outsiders who will be ever unable to ask the native, since the natives are long gone.

When we translate, our translations must necessarily be colored by our particular understanding or Old Norse mythology and the emphasis we have on what is important to convey. Thus we are often left with guesswork – although some guesswork is more educated and based on more evidence than others. Adding to the fact that all translators are really interpreters, we must also ask ourselves how we want to offer our translation. Some translators will try to recreate what they believe to be the rhythmic, ceremonious experience that the ancient audience may have felt. In order to make the poetry sound right in a modern language, one obviously has to adapt the text and the choice of words. Others may try to emphasize the archaic aspect of this poetry by using old- fashioned or lofty, "Shakespearean" language.

Others again, like myself, may emphasize what we believe the poet was trying to tell us, and try to make it as easily available to the audience as possible. I have found that the best possible way to translate, is to be as literal as possible. Thus I have offered the Old Norse text next to my translations, so that the reader may see each line both in the ancient text and in the modern translation. I have, as far as it is possible, translated each line directly, without making changes to the original form. I have found that it is possible to do so and still let the English translation sound good poetically. What makes my translation most particular compared with other translations is that I have always and without exception offered translations of mythical names.

It was my most important discovery, when trying to decipher the myths, that the names of characters, the names of things and the names of places all carry meaning: Meaning crucial to our understanding of the messages that are being conveyed through poetry and mythology. The poems are stripped of their essential meaning when the reader is left with foreign names that only appear to be meaningless syllables. The names have a function in the myths; they are that which truly indicates what the myth is really about. The Old Norse audience who listened to this poetry all understood the meaning and the double or even triple meanings of the names presented in mythological poetry. When modern translators ignore these meanings and fail to offer translations or interpretations of names in mythical poetry, they are taking the real meaning of the myths away from the modern reader, who can only accept the translations offered.

I cannot say whether this failure to offer name-translations is done because of a lack of understanding their importance, or whether it is simply a fear to take a chance and offer an interpretation to a name which is often a much discussed subject. The latter is quite understandable: Many mythical names have a meaning that seems obscure to us today. The way the names were written down in a time before the rules of writing the Old Norse language was fully settled often in itself renders the names ambiguous, since we have to choose which of the two rather similar words were really meant. Sometimes the names are of a very ancient origin, belonging, really, to earlier stages of the language or lent from foreign languages or dialects. The poets, however, were in my opinion obviously aware of their meaning.

Sometimes, the words that make up a name (usually two) seem straightforward enough, but do not seem to make sense to the modern mind. However, it is my experience that even when a name appears obscure at first, it makes sense through closer scrutiny and comparisons with other myths, other entities, and their functions. One such "weird" name is, for example, the name Hænir, which actually translates as "chicken" in the plural. As the supreme giver of intelligence and thought to men and women, the name appears undignified and weird, but no other possible meaning can be applied to it. The god is one of the many whose role is entirely poetical and who does not appear to have ever been worshiped in the Heathen cults, so that his name indicates something crucial about his function and its message within the myth.

Through my own studies of Old Norse myths, I realized that the thinking mind is often the object of ridicule in the myths, especially as it strives desperately to keep up a limited perception of the word. The theme reminds me of various ancient techniques of meditation which teach the importance of silencing the mind, describing the thinking mind as an endless, internal monologue that maintains our ideas about the world and about ourselves, but which easily keeps us apart from our true, spiritual selves. When the chatter of the mind is silenced, the true seeing mind can open its eye and see through illusion. Thus when the giver of thoughts is called "Chicken", we may imagine the incessant clucking noise of a herd of chicken as a perfect and humorous description of how the thinking mind actually works. This use of subtle riddles and meaningful humor is typical of Norse poetry.

This is why I have chosen to render the direct translation, although it may sound funny and awkward until we think about it. In this translation of the Vǫluspá, there are only a very few names which are not translated throughout: The name Óðinn, which actually translates as "The Spirit", "The Poetry" or "The Frenzy". The name Frigg, related to words for ruling powers, love, wisdom and fertility. The name Þórr, which is related to "Thunder", the name Loki, whose meaning is obscure, and the name Baldr, which means "Bold". I mostly left these names in their Old Norse form because these characters carry so many associations.

As a rule, you could say that Óðinn always represents the learning spirit within everything, Frigg represents the silent knowledge within as well as love as a power, Þórr represents the thinking mind (as does "Chicken"), while Baldr represents the bold freedom and generosity of an open, objective mind. Loki represents first and foremost the power that propels conflict, which is necessary in all dramas, but also the passion and fiery life-force that may be both destructive and constructive. Most other names, including Óðin´s many nicknames, are rendered in their translated and/or interpreted form. For reasons described above, some of the translations are choices I have had to make between different known interpretations or interpretations of my own.

All are based on years of research and reconsiderations, and found by me to be the best interpretation when the whole of the Edda lore is seen as one great context. I often leave a little explanation of my translations in the footnotes, especially when they differ severely from the norm. I have found Rudolf Simek´s Dictionary of Northern Mythology very helpful, since Simek´s work compiles various interpretations of names made by different Norse linguists over the last century or so, and even when my own interpretations take a different turn, these have provided me with alternatives, comparisons and suggestions.

VǪLUSPÁ
THE DIVINATION OF THE WITCH

ABOUT THE VǪLUSPÁ

The poem Vǫluspá is one of the most famous poems found in the collection of Norse Heathen, Viking Age mythical poems popularly known as the Poetic Edda. It tells the story of the universe from creation to destruction, laid in the mouth of a wise woman performing a séance of oracular divination known to the Old Norse Heathens as seiðr. It was an art that held much in common both with shamanism, witchcraft and ancient European oracular traditions, an art much revered by Norse Heathens. In this poem, we are presented with a traditional setting for oracular seiðr, and the woman who transmits the prophecy uses the poetic language of allusive metaphors as she looks to the past, the present, and the likely future. To divine past, present and future – not just as an oracular divination but often with the purpose of actively altering fate – was an important part of seiðr.

The poem Vǫluspá describes such a séance of oracular divination, where the witch addresses a universal audience after having been, as was the tradition, paid and asked by the lord of the hall, in this case the god Óðinn. From other sources describing such séances, we know that use of poetry and allegory was also how the messages of the divination were transmitted in Heathen times. The priestess would be seated on a chair or a platform, surrounded by all the people of the residence that she had visited. She would be treated with the utmost reverence during her stay, but she herself would treat everybody as equals, no matter how high or how low their birth. She would perform rituals that called upon helping spirits who could show her how to proceed.

The sagas describe traveling priestesses – sometimes traveling in groups of nine, other times traveling alone, or accompanied and assisted by male and female apprentices. Older, Latin sources about the tribes of the continent describe female oracles seated on high platforms, even small towers, while their message was voiced through an intermediary who spoke the prophecies through the language of poetry. One saga, Eiriks saga Rauða, describes a ritual feast and how the women of the residence held hands and formed a circle around the priestess while singing an invocation called varðlokur – "Invoke the Spirits".

When the spirits arrived, the priestess could see what "had before been hidden", and provide divination for everybody present. The men remained outside of the circle, observing, and it is true that many sources indicate that although seiðr was practiced by certain men and known by some, it was primarily the sphere of women. In the Edda lore, there are a few other poems that also take the form of a séance of seiðr: The Hyndluljóð ("Song of Hyndla"), Vegtamskvíða ("Song of Way-Wont" or "Baldrs Dreams"), Gróagaldr ("Gróa´s Spell-songs") and the Grípisspá ("The Prophecy of Grípir"). The latter is the only poem where a man performs the seiðr, and the name Grípir is a disguise for Óðinn.

The title Vǫluspá has been translated in various manners: "The Song of the Sibyl", "The Prophecy of the Seeress", or as I have chosen, "The Divination of the Witch". The title is derived from two words: -spá, which means "divination" or "prophecy", and vǫlu- which is genitive singular of the feminine singular noun vǫlva. Vǫlva was the professional title of a female practitioner of the art of seiðr in the Old Norse Heathen religion. The title literally translates as "wed to the wand" – the wand being the symbol of the sacred office of the vǫlva. The art of seiðr often took the form of divination and prophecy, associating it with the oracular traditions of Heathen Europe. However, seiðr was more than divination, and its practitioners knew more than divination, so that the interpretation "sibyl" or "seeress" becomes, in my opinion, too narrow.

The word priestess could be adequate, seeing what role these vǫlur played in the official religious life of Norse Heathens, yet there is little evidence for an organized priestess-hood – although the lack of evidence does not mean there was no such thing. We just do not know. Looking at the art of seiðr as it is described in the sources as well as the cultural- religious role of the vǫlva, I believe the best interpretation of her title is "witch" – seen from the point of view of a tradition where witches and witchcraft were time- honored institutions demanding respect, even reverence. A witch in the Heathen context was not a nasty wart-nosed creature out to eat small children but a wise woman with access to the knowledge of the goddesses of fate. Numerous sources indicate that Viking Age Scandinavians revered such women and frequently sought their counsel. In the case of the Vǫluspá witch, she is also a divine or supernatural and extremely ancient creature who remembers a time before the present universe existed.

The Edda poem Vǫluspá has been transmitted to us by three different written sources. The oldest known version was rendered in its entirety in the Codex Regius manuscript, whose author or editor remains unknown although it has been suggested that the writer of the original manuscript from which the Codex was copied has been written down by the monk Sæmundr "The Wise" Fróði (1056- 1153). Parts of the poem are also rendered in Snorri Sturluson´s (1179-1241) Prose Edda. Another full version was presented by Haukr Erlendsson (d.1334) in his Hauksbók. There are some variations between the three versions of the poem, mostly linguistic variations and spellings. The rules of spelling had not been laid down strictly. However, the differences are slight. In 1867, the Norwegian linguist Sophus Bugge let present all three versions as well as a "normalized" text based on all the three versions. This normalized text is the version I use when I translate the text of the Vǫluspá. All the Old Norse versions may be read in Bugge´s work, available online at http://etext.old.no/ .

The poem was probably transmitted orally before it was written down, but no one knows how old it is or who composed it, and whether it is the original composition of the poem that we are presented with in the written sources. A strong case has been made for the poem originating in the Lade court of Norway towards the end of the Viking Age, composed by Heathens who were at war with the new religion (Christianity) and its promoters. Composing a poem that divined and described basic Heathen cosmology may have been part of a campaign to strengthen the old faith.

The Divination of The Witch

The Wand-Witch spoke:

1. "Attention I demand from all
the sacred families;
greater and lesser children of
Great World;
You want me, Val-Father,
to give a good account
of the most ancient tales
that which I remember best."

Vǫlva kvað:

1. «Hljóðs bið ek allar helgar
kindir,
meiri ok minni mǫgu Heimdallar;
viltu, at ek, Valfǫðr! vel framtelja
forn spjǫll fíra,
þau er fremst um man.

2. I remember giants
born before time
those who in the olden days had
me fostered
Nine worlds I remember Nine
Witches Within Wood Before the
Mead-Tree sprouted from the
ground below.

2. Ec man iotna ár um borna
þa er fordom
mic fodda hofdo
Nio man æc heima
Nío Iviði
Miotuið moran fyr mold nedan.

3. In the beginning was the Wave
where Sound built
There was neither sand nor sea,
nor cool little waves
Earth was not, nor heaven above
The Open Mouth of the Sacred
Descendants was yet no growth.

3. Ár var alda
Þar er Ymir bygði
vara sandr né sær né svalar unnir,
Jǫrð fannsk æva né upphiminn,
Gap var Ginnunga, en gras hvergi.

4. Before the sons of Storage
Chamber lifted up the lands
they who shaped
the precious Middle World
Sun shone from the south
on the rocks of the hall [=Earth]
then the Earth began to grow the
green plants. [6]

4. Áðr Burs synir bjǫðum um
ypðu, þeir er Miðgarð mœran
skópu
Sól skein sunnan á salar steina,
þá var Grund gróin grœnum lauki.

5. Sun hurled from the south
together with Moon;
She threw her right hand around
the Door of the Steeds of Heaven
Sun knew not
where she owned her halls Moon
knew not
what power he possessed the stars
knew not
where they owned their places.[7]

5. Sól varp sunnan, sinni Mána,
hendi inni hœgri um Himinjódyr
Sól þat ne vissi hvar hon sali átti,
Máni þat ne vissi
hvat hann megins átti, stjǫrnur
þat ne vissu hvar þær staði áttu.

6. Then all the powers went to the
high Chairs of Fate the sacrosanct
gods
to discuss this;
to Night and her kindred did they
give names
There would be a Morning and a
Midday
Afternoon and Evening to reckon
the years. [8]

6. Þá gengu regin ǫll á rǫkstóla,
ginnheilug goð,
ok um þat gættusk;
Nátt ok niðjum nǫfn um gáfu,
Morgin hétu
ok Miðjan Dag, Undorn ok Aptan,
árum at telja.

7. The Aesir met up at the
Field of Streams Returning to
Watersource THEY raised altars
and high temples
They set up their forges
They forged the precious trea-
sures They shaped tongs
and they made tools.[9]

8. They played chequers in the
meadow They were joyful then
They were content and knew no
lack of Gold[10]
Until Three [females] came there
- trolls´ maidens -
they were powerful, all-mighty,
from the Giant World.[11]

9. Then all the powers went to the
high Chairs of Fate the sacrosanct
gods
to discuss this;
Who owed the King of Dwarfs to
be shaped
from the blood of Fire
and the limbs of the Dead?[12]

10. Then was Shape-Searcher the
greatest and the highest of all
dwarfs
and Sleeper was the second (in
rank);
Images of humans they made
many of
from earth, these dwarfs as the
Sleeper spoke it.[13]

11. Waxing, Waning, Northern,
Southern Eastern, Western,
Ale-Thief, Hibernation Death and
Dying,
Close-Call and Dead One Shaking,
Vibration,
Bom-Tree, Ship Friend and Other
One, Frightened One, Mead-Wit-
ness [14]

7. Hittusk æsir á Iðavǫllr , þeir er
hǫrg
ok hof hátimbruðu, afla lǫgðu,
auð smíðuðu, tangir skópu ok tól
gǫrðu.

8. Tefldu í túni, teitir váru,
var þeim vettugis vant ór Gull
unz þrjár kvámu þursa meyjar
ámátkar mjǫk ór Jǫtunheimum

9. Þá gengu regin ǫll á rǫkstóla,
ginnheilug goð,
ok um þat gættusk:
hverr skyldi Dverga Drótt um
skepja
ór Brimi blóðgu
ok ór Bláins leggjum

10. Þar var Móðsognir mæztr um
orðinn dverga allra,
en Durinn annarr;
þeir mannlíkun mǫrg um gǫrðu
dvergar í jǫrðu, sem Durinn sagði.

11. Nýi, Niði,
Norðri, Suðri, Austri, Vestri,
Alþjófr, Dvalinn, Nár ok Náinn,
Nípingr, Dáinn, Bifurr, Bafurr,
Bǫmburr, Nori, Ánn ok Ánarr,
Óinn.
Mjǫðvitnir

12. Power Drink and Magic Wand
Elf, Wind-Elf [=Mortal Soul]
Daring One, Yearning and Desir-
ing One
Appreciated, Color, Wisdom Re-
newal and New Counsel,
Now I have the dwarfs, Ruler and
Counsel Wise, rightly counted.[15]

13. Hiding, Wedge,
Found One, Needle-Sized Shaft,
Intent,
Skillful One, Burner, Twin,
Bushy-Browed, Blood-Knife,
Chamber, Quick One, Horn-Blow-
er, Famous, Lazy/Shining
Out-of-Falseness/Gravel Field
Quarrelsome, Crazy Shields[16]

14. It is time to count
the dwarfs of Hibernation
to count the people of the Law:
They set out from the rocky halls
from the Gravel Fields
to the Fields of Earth:[17]

15. There was Dripper and Hid-
den Tracker
High One, Burial Mound-Spurrer,
Wind-Shielded (=immortal) Field
Glowing One
Fool, Snake, Sleepy, Alert Spirit
Cut-Out-Part, Dyer,
Part-Finder, Great Grandfather[18]

16. Elf [=Soul] and Sacred Youth,
Crazy Shields
Spy and Frosty,
Finder and Sacred Warrior;
As long as human kind exists
the long list of the Laws shall be
remembered.[19]

17. Until Three [males] came out
of that flock [of dwarfs]: Powerful
and loving
Aesir to the homes
They found on the shore, of little
power
Ask and Embla without destiny.[20]

12. Veigr ok Gandálfr, Vindálfr,
Þorinn, Þrár ok Þráinn,
Þekkr, Litr ok Vitr, Nýr ok Nýráðr,
nú hefi ek dverga, Reginn ok
Ráðsviðr, rétt um talða.

13. Fili, Kili,
Fundinn, Nali, Hepti, Vili,
Hanarr, Svíurr, Billingr, Brúni,
Bildr ok Buri, Frár, Hornbori,
Frægr ok Lóni, Aurvangr,
Jari, Eikinskjaldi.

14. Mál er dverga i Dvalins liði
ljóna kindum i Lofars telja:
er sóttu frá salar steini Aurvanga
sjǫt
til Jǫruvalla.

15. Þar var Draupnir
ok Dólgþrasir, Hár, Haugspori,
Hlévangr, Glóinn,
Dori, Ori, Dúfr, Andvari,
Skirfir, Virfir, Skafiðr, Ai.

16. Álfr ok Yngvi, Eikinskjaldi,
Fjalarr ok Frosti, Finnr ok Gin-
narr;
þat man æ uppi, meðan ǫld lifir,
langniðja tal Lofars hafat.

17. Unz þrír kvámu
ór því liði: ǫflgir ok ástkir æsir á
húsi
fundu á landi lítt megandi Ask ok
Emblu, ǫrlǫgslausa.

18. They had no breath/spirit
They had no poetry/mind they
had no vitality
no beautiful colors;
Óðinn gave them breath/spirit
Chicken gave them poetry/mind
The Heat gave them vitality and
beautiful colors.[21]

19. I know an ash stands
It is called the Old Steed a tall
tree, poured over
with shining bright gravel;
From there comes the dew that
falls in the valleys
It stands ever green above the
Well of Origin.[22]

20. From there [the Well of Ori-
gin] come maidens
possessing much knowledge:
Three [maidens], from that hall
which stands beneath the Tree
Origin, the first is called
the second Is About To Happen
they carved [runes] into the wood,
Debt was the third [maiden];
They made the laws
They shaped the lives
For the children of the ages they
determined all fate.[23]

21. She remembers
the first war in the world When
Gold Power-Drink was hoist on
the spears
and in the High One`s hall they
burned her;
Three times they burned the
Three Times Born often, not
seldom
yet she still lives![24]

22. She was called Bright One
when she came to the settlements
The well-divining witch
She could cast spells
she did seiðr wherever she could
she did seiðr with a playful intent
She was always loved by wicked/
ill women.[25]

18. Ǫnd þau ne áttu, óð þau ne
hǫfðu, lá né læti
né litu góða;
ǫnd gaf Óðinn, óð gaf Hœnir, lá
gaf Lóður ok litu góða

19. Ask veit ek standa, heitir Yggdrasill hár baðmr, ausinn hvíta
auri;
þaðan koma dǫggvar þærs í dala
falla; stendr æ yfir grœnn Urðar
Brunni.

20. Þaðan koma meyjar margs
vitandi þrjár, ór þeim sal er und
þolli stendr;
Urð hétu eina, aðra Verðandi,
skáru á skíði,
Skuld ina þriðju;
þær lǫg lǫgðu, þær líf kuru alda
bǫrnum, ǫrlǫg seggja.

21. Þat man hon
fólkvíg fyrst í heimi, er Gullveigr
geirum studdu
ok í hǫll Hárs hana brendu;
þrysvar brendu þrysvar borna,
opt, ósjaldan, þó hon enn lifir!

22. Heiði hana hétu, hvars til húsa
kom, vǫlu velspá,
vitti hon ganda,
seið hon hvars hon kunni, seið
hon hugleikin,
æ var hon angan illrar brúðar.

23. Then all the rulers went to the high Chairs of Fate the sacrosanct gods
to discuss this:
Ought the Aesir alone owe to suffer the loss,
or ought all the gods together owe to pay the debt/atonement?[26]

24. Óðinn hurled [his spear] and shot against the people there was a war,
the first in the world;
Broken were the wooden walls of the Aesir strongholds
the Vanir, victorious, openly swarmed the fields.[27]

25. Then all the powers went to the high Chairs of Fate the sacrosanct gods
to discuss this:
Who had blended the air all with harm?
Or to the devourers´ kind given Poetry´s Maiden?[28]

26. Þórr was then the only one striking seized by anger,
he seldom sits
when he hears such things;
Oaths were broken then words and promises
all the powerful words
that had passed between them.[29]

27. She knows that Great World´s listening attention is disguised beneath the bright radiant sacred tree;
She sees a torrent of water poured mixed with mud-gravel
from the Val-Father´s wager: Do you understand now, or what?[30]

23. Þá gengu regin ǫll á Rǫkstóla,
ginnheilug goð,
ok um þat gættusk;
Hvárt skyldu æsir afráð gjalda,
eða skyldu goðin ǫll gildi eiga.

24. Fleygði Óðinn
ok í fólk um skaut, þat var enn
fólkvíg fyrst í heimi;
brotinn var borðveggr borgar ása,
knáttu vanir vígská vǫllu sporna.

25. Þá gengu regin ǫll á rǫkstóla,
ginnheilug goð,
ok um þat gættusk:
hverr hefði lopt allt lævi blandit
eða ætt jǫtuns Óðs mey gefna

26. Þórr einn þar vá þrunginn
móði, hann sjaldan sitr
er hann slíkt um fregn;
á gengust eiðar, orð ok sœri,
mál ǫll meginlig er á meðal fóru

27. Veit hon Heimdallar hljóð um
fólgit undir heiðvǫnum helgum baðmi;
á sér hon ausask aurgum forsi
af veði Valfǫðrs.
Vituð ér enn eða hvat?

28. She sat outside alone when
the Aged One came
the Old-Young of the Aesir and
their eyes met:
"Why do you ask me? Why do you
test me?
I know everything, Óðinn! Where
you hid your eye: in the famous
Well of Memory:
Memory drinks the mead every
morning
from the Val-Father´s wager." Do
you understand now, or what?[31]

29. For her, the Father of Hosts
chose rings and jewels
for her wise speech
and her magical divination:
She saw widely, so widely into all
the worlds[32]

30. She saw valkyriur widely ar-
riving ready to ride to the Divine
peoples:
Debt held a shield, and Battle
another
War, Fighting and Magician and
Spear Battle;
Now are they counted, the women
of the Ruler;
valkyriur ready to ride the Earth[33]

31. I saw for Baldr,
the bloodied/sacrificed god,
Spirit´s child, his fate concealed:
There stood on the hill,
grown above the plain
the mistletoe, slender and very
fair.[34]

32. There was from that wood
which seemed so frail
an arrow of sorrow, and Strife
shot it.
Baldr´s brother
was quick being born so Óðin´s
son began
fighting at one night old.[35]

28. Ein sat hon úti, þá er Inn
Aldni kom Yggjungr ása
ok í augu leit:
"Hvers fregnið mik? hví freistið
mín?
alt veit ek, Óðinn! hvar þú auga
falt: í inum mœra Mímis brunni;
drekkr mjǫð Mímir morgin
hverjan
af veði Valfǫðrs." Vituð ér enn eða
hvat?

29. Valði henni Herfǫðr hringa ok
men, féspjǫll spaklig
ok spáganda;
sá hon vítt ok um vítt of verǫld
hverja.

30. Sá hon valkyrjur vítt um
komnar
gǫrvar at ríða til Goðþjóðar:
Skuld hélt skildi, en Skǫgul
ǫnnur,
Gunnr, Hildr, Gǫndul ok
Geirskǫgul;
nú eru talðar nǫnnur Herjans,
gǫrvar at ríða grund valkyrjur

31. Ek sá Baldri, blóðgum tívur,
Óðins barni ǫrlǫg fólgin: stóð um
vaxinn
vǫllum hæri
mjór ok mjǫk fagr mistilteinn.

32. Varð af þeim meiði, er mér
sýndisk, harmflaug hættlig, Hǫðr
nam skjóta.
Baldrs bróðir
var of borinn snemma, sá nam
Óðins sonr einnættr vega.

33. He washed not his hands
nor combed he his hair until he
brought to the pyre the killer of
Baldr´s spirit.
And Frigg wept in the Moist Halls
for the woe of Valhǫll
Do you understand now, or
what?[36]

33. Þó hann æva hendr né hǫfuð
kembði,
áðr á bál um bar Baldrs andskota.
En Frigg um grét í Fensǫlum
vá Valhallar.
Vituð ér enn eða hvat?

34. Then were twisted
the war-bonds of Choice the
rather hardened ones made of
entrails.[37]

34. Þá kná Vala vígbǫnd snúa,
heldr váru harðgǫr hǫpt ór þǫr-
mum

35. She saw a captive lie
beneath the Grove of Cauldrons
Loki´s harmful likeness she recognized;
There sits Victory Woman, very
unhappy Unhappy with her
husband.
Do you understand now, or
what?[38]

35. Hapt sá hon liggja undir
Hvera Lundi lægjarnlíki Loka
áþekkjan;
þar sitr Sigyn þeygi um sínum ver
vel glýjuð.
Vituð ér enn eða hvat?

36. A river falls from the east
through the poisonous valleys full
of knives and swords
she is called Sharp One.[39]

36. Á fellr austan
um eitrdala
sǫxum ok sverðum, Slíðr heitir sú

37. Stood to the North on the
Waning Plains
a hall of gold, owned by
the lineage of Glowing Spark;
Another stood
at the Never Cooling place, the
beer-hall of the Devourer who is
called Fire.[40]

37. Stóð fyr norðan á Niðavǫllum
salr ór gulli Sindra ættar;
en annarr stóð á Ókólni, bjórsalr
Jǫtuns,
en sá Brímir heitir.

38. She sees a hall standing far
from the Sun
on the Shore of Corpses - To the
North that door is facing;
Poisonous drops fall
in through the roof-vents That
hall is woven
from the spines of serpents.[41]

38. Sal sá hon standa Sólu fjarri
Nástrǫndu á, norðr horfa dyrr;
féllu eitrdropar inn um ljóra,
sá er undinn salr orma hryggjum.

39. There she saw wading in
heavy currents
oath-breakers greed- murderers
and those who by force take the
beloveds of others.
There sucks the Shame Biter from
their dead rotting bodies and
wolves tear them.
Do you understand now, or
what?[42]

40. To the East sat The Old One
in Iron Forest
nurtures there birth
to the kindred of Greed;
From all of these
one of darkness comes Moon´s
abductor
in the shape of a troll.[43]

41. It drinks the life-power of men
wed to death
It colors the halls of rulers with
crimson blood;
Black is the Sun´s shine the
summer that follows the weather
all cruel.
Do you understand yet, or what?[44]

42. Sat there on the mound playing his harp
the herdsman of the giantesses-
the happy Sharp Edge-Servant;
A rooster crowed
in the Gallows-Wood the fair red
rooster
who is called Deceiver.[45]

43. Crowed for the Aesir Golden
Comb
who wakes the warriors of the
Father of Rulers;
Another crows
from beneath the Earth a soot-red
rooster
in the halls of Hel. [46]

39. Sá hon þar vaða þunga strau-
ma menn meinsvara
ok morðvarga
ok þanns annars glepr eyrarúnu;
þar saug Níðhǫggr nái framgeng-
na, sleit vargr vera.
Vituð ér enn eða hvat?

40. Austr sat in aldna í Járnviði
ok fœddi þar Fenris kindir;
verðr af þeim ǫllum einna nǫk-
kurr Tungls tjúgari
í trolls hami.

41. Fyllisk fjǫrvi feigra manna,
rýðr ragna sjǫt rauðum dreyra;
svǫrt verða Sólskin um sumur
eptir, veðr ǫll válynd.
Vituð ér enn eða hvat?

42. Sat þar á haugi ok sló hǫrpu
gýgjar hirðir
glaðr Egðir;
gól um hánum í gaglviði fagr-
rauðr hani,
sá er Fjalarr heitir.

43. Gól um ásum Gullinkambi,
sá vekr hǫlða at Herjafǫðrs;
En annarr gelr fyr jǫrð neðan
sótrauðr hani
at sǫlum Heljar.

44. Gluttony barks loudly before
the Protruding Cave the fastening
bond is torn and Greed runs free.
She knows many tidings,
I see even further
about the Fall of the Rulers
and the doom of victorious gods.[47]

44. Geyr Garmr mjǫk fyr Gnípahelli;
festr man slitna, en Freki renna.
Fjǫld veit hon frœða, fram sé ek
lengra, um Ragnarǫk
rǫmm sigtíva.

45. Brothers will fight their
own brothers and be their kin´s
slayers
children of sisters will betray their
relations:
Hardness is in the world, prosti-
tution abounds, axe age, sword
age, shields are cleft asunder
wind [death] age, wolf [greed]
age,
Before all the world plunges no
man will spare another. [48]

45. Brœðr munu berjask ok at
bǫnum verðask, munu systrungar
sifjum spilla;
Hart er í heimi, hórdómr mikill,
skeggjǫld, skálmǫld, skildir 'ru
klofnir,
vindǫld, vargǫld,
áðr verǫld steypisk; man engi
maðr ǫðrum þyrma.

46. The sons of Memory play
and the Mead-Wave catches fire
at the ancient
Bellowing Horn;
Hard blows the Great World the
horn raised high: -Spirit speaks
with the head of Memory. [49]

46. Leika Míms synir, en Mjǫtuðr
kyndisk, at inu gamla Gjallarhor-
ni;
hátt blæss Heimdallr,
-horn er á lopti; - mælir Óðinn
við Míms hǫfuð.

47. The Old Steed shivers
the standing [= present] ash [=
universe] the ancient tree sounds,
and the Devourer is loose;
All are terrified
on the Road to Death
before the kin of the Sooty One
swallows the sleepers up.[50]

47. Skelfr Yggdrasils askr stan-
dandi,
ymr it aldna tré, en jǫtunn losnar;
hræðask allir
á Helvegum, áðr Surtar þann sefi
of gleypir.

48.What about the Aesir?
What about the elves [souls of the
dead]? The World of Devourers
groans,
The Aesir are at parliament;
The dwarfs howl
before their rocky doors
these wise ones of the rock walls
Do you understand yet, or what?[51]

48. Hvat er með ásum? hvat er
með álfum? gnýr allr jǫtunheimr,
æsir 'ru á þingi;
stynja dvergar fyr steindurum
veggbergs vísir.
Vituð ér enn eða hvat?

49. Gluttony barks loudly before
the Protruding Cave the fastening
bond is torn and Greed runs free.
52

49. Geyr nú Garmr mjǫk fyr
Gnípahelli;
festr man slitna, en freki renna.

50. Weakening comes from the
East before him his shield
Great Magic twists
in the Rage of the Devourer:
The serpent churns the waves and
the eagle shrieks
the corpses are torn
and Nail-Traveler is loose.⁵³

51. A ship comes from the East
Now may arrive the people of
Muspell over the waves
steered by Loki;
There are all the monstrous com-
panions of Greed,
with them the brother of Wind
Lightning⁵⁴

52. The Sooted One travels from
the South with scorching fires
from the sword shines
the Sun of the gods of the Choice
The rocky wall falls
and the troll women hurl; humans
walk the Road to Death and the
heaven is torn asunder.⁵⁵

53. Then comes Tranquility´s [=
Frigg´s] second sorrow forth:
when Óðinn marches
to fight the wolf [of Greed]
And the Slayer of the Bellower [=
Freyr] brightly braves the Sooty
One;
Then must fall
Frigg´s pleasure [= Óðinn/
Freyr].⁵⁶

54. Gluttony barks loudly before
the Protruding Cave the fastening bond is torn and Greed runs
free.⁵⁷

55. Then comes the powerful Son
of Victory Father:
The Expander to fight the Beast of
Choice:
He lets the son of the Roarer´s
line be stabbed, the sword
shoved all the way into its heart;
thus is the father avenged.⁵⁸

50. Hrymr ekr Austan, hefisk lind
fyrir.
Snýsk jǫrmungandr í Jǫtunmóði:
Ormr knýr unnir, en ari hlakkar,
slítr nái niðfǫlr. Naglfar losnar.

51. Kjóll ferr Austan, koma munu
Muspells um lǫg lýðir,
en Loki stýrir;
Fara fíflmegir með Freka allir,
þeim er bróðir Byleists í fǫr.

52. Surtr ferr Sunnan með sviga
lævi,
skínn af sverði Sól Valtíva.
Grjótbjǫrg gnata, en gífr hrata;
troða halir Helveg, en himinn
klofnar.

53.Þá kemr Hlínar harmr annarr
fram, er Óðinn ferr
við úlf vega,
en bani Belja bjartr at Surti; þar
man Friggjar falla angan.

54. Geyr nú Garmr mjǫk fyr
Gnípahelli;
festr man slitna, en freki renna.

55. Þá kemr inn mikli mǫgr
Sigfǫður:
Viðarr vega at Valdýri;
lætr hann megi hveðrungs mund
um standa
hjǫr til hjarta; þá er hefnt fǫður.

56. Then comes the glorious son
of Heat Woman [Earth]
Óðin´s son [Þórr] goes to fight the
serpent:
in wrath he strikes,
the Protector of the Middle World
[= Þórr],
All humans must now leave their
homesteads:
He walks the Nine Steps,
the son of Life Struggle [Earth],
death-wed he is
yet no scorn will be spoken [of
him now]⁵⁹

56. Þá kemr inn mœri mǫgr
Hlóðynjar gengr Óðins sonr við
orm vega;
drepr hann af móði Miðgarðs
véurr;
munu halir allir heimstǫð ryðja;
gengr Fet Níu Fjǫrgynjar burr
neppr frá naðri níðs ókvíðnum.

57. The Sun is blackened Earth
sinks into the ocean disappearing
from the heavens the bright stars
steam rises op from huge fires,
a high flame plays against heaven
itself.⁶⁰

57. Sól tér sortna, sígr fold í mar,
hverfa af himni heiðar stjǫrnur;
geisar eimi
ok aldrnari, leikr hár hiti
við himin sjálfan.

58. Gluttony barks loudly before
the Protruding Cave the fastening bond is torn and Greed runs
free.⁶¹

58. Geyr nú Garmr mjǫk
fyr Gnípahelli; festr man slitna,
en freki renna.

59. She sees, coming up a second
time,
Earth from the Ocean eternally
green:
waterfalls rushing the eagle soars
above
the one who in the mountains
hunts the fish.⁶²

59. Sér hon upp koma ǫðru sinni
Jǫrð ór Ægi iðjagrœna;
falla forsar, flýgr ǫrn yfir, sá er á
fjalli fiska veiðir.

60. The Aesir find themselves on
the
Plains of the Streams Returning to Source and about the
Earth-girdler
they discuss
and there they remember the
great events
and the Great Sage´s ancient
runes.⁶³

60. Finnask æsir á Iðavelli
ok um Moldþinur mátkan dœma
ok minnask þar á megindóma ok
á Fimbultýs fornar rúnar.

61. There shall, afterwards the
wonderful
golden chequers
be found in the grass:
the ones that in the times of old
they had possessed.⁶⁴

61. Þar munu eptir undrsamligar
gullnar tǫflur
í grasi finnask,
þærs í árdaga áttar hǫfðu.

62. Unsown may
the fields grow fertile
all sicknesses will be healed, and
Baldr will return:
They will live together, Strife and
Baldr on the battlefield of the
Shattered One the great gods of
Choice.
Do you understand yet, or what?[65]

63. Then will Chicken [the human
Mind] choose wooden sticks
for divination and the sons of
brothers
will inhabit together
the Wide World of Winds.
Do you understand yet, or what?[66]

64. She sees a hall standing as fair
as the Sun
with golden roofs
at Shielded from Fire;
There shall deceit-free rulers
build
and for all eternity enjoy their
happiness.[67]

65. Then comes the powerful one
ruler of everything
emerging from above the one who
rules all.[68]

66. Then comes the dragon of
darkness flying
The shining serpent ascending
from the Waning/Shame Hills
In his wings he carries corpses he
flies across the plains –
Waning/Shame Biter and his
corpses. Now she wishes to
sink."[69]

62. Munu ósánir akrar vaxa,
bǫls man alls batna, Baldr man
koma;
búa þeir Hǫðr ok Baldr Hropts
sigtoptir
vel valtívar.
Vituð ér enn eða hvat?

63. Þá kná Hœnir hlut við kjósa
ok burir byggja brœðra tveggja
Vindheim víðan.
Vituð ér enn eða hvat?

64. Sal sér hon standa sólu fegra
gulli þakðan á Gimlé;
þar skulu dyggvar dróttir byggja
ok um aldrdaga ynðis njóta.

65. Þá kemr inn ríki at regindómi
ǫflugr ofan,
sá er ǫllu ræðr.

66. Þar kemr inn dimmi dreki
fljúgandi,
naðr fránn neðan frá Niðafjǫllum;
berr sér í fjǫðrum
— flýgr vǫll yfir — Niðhǫggr nái.
Nú man hon sǫkkvask.»

VAFÞRÚÐNISMÁL

The Speech Of The Powerful Head-Veil

Vafþrúðnismál is a cosmology poem taking the shape of a
word-duel between Óðinn and the giant Vafþrúðnir. His name
is derived from váf, meaning a head- veil, and þrúðnir, which
means "powerful", "tremendous". Óðinn, of course, represents
the Spirit, seeking knowledge, but not just for the sake of knowledge; he wants to see how this "head-veil" has "made his halls".
From many other stories we may deduce that the giant represents
illusion, what constitutes the material world, and that the duel is
about Spirit trying to get out alive. The idea that the whole world is
illusion, or a story told, is evident in many other stories, such as in
Snorri´s Gylfaginning (The Illusions of the Sorcerer). In that story,
the sorcerer king, Gylfi, travels to the world of the gods, where he
is invited, exactly, to a word duel.

It would almost seem that these duels described in Edda poetry
are similar to a kind of examination of aspiring skalds who have
to enter a hall of peers and prove himself worthy of becoming a
skald:

"He[Gylfi] saw three high-seats, each above the other, and
three men sat thereon,-one on each. And he asked what
might be the name of those lords. He who had conducted
him in answered that the one who sat on the nethermost
high-seat was a king, "and his name is High, but the next
is named Equally High, and he who is uppermost is called
Third. Then High asked the newcomer whether his er-
rand were more than for the meat and drink which were
always at his command, as for every one there in the Hall
of the High One. He answered that he first desired to learn
whether there were any wise man there within. High said
that he should not escape whole from thence unless he
were wiser; "And stand forth, the one who asks. The one
who answers shall sit."

After having asked and been told the entire history of cosmos, the High declares:

"But now, if you are able to ask yet further, then indeed I know not from where answer shall come to you, for I never heard any man tell forth at greater length the course of the world; and now avail yourself of that which you have heard."

Thereupon Gangleri [Wandering Learning = Gylfi] heard great noises on every side of him; and then, when he had looked about him more, lo, he stood out of doors on a level plain, and saw no hall there and no castle. Then he went his way forth and came home into his kingdom, and told those tidings which he had seen and heard; and after him each man told these tales to the other.

But the Æsir sat them down to speak together, and took counsel and recalled all these tales which had been told to him. And they gave these same names that were named before to those men and places that were there, to the end that when long ages should have passed away.

In short, the world is a story told after a vision, and becoming real by the telling and the retelling.

THE SPEECH OF THE POWERFUL HEAD-VEIL
ROUND ONE BEGINS

1. Oðinn said:
"Advise me now, Frigg, for I intend to journey
to visit the Powerful Head-Veil
I have a great interest
in contending over ancient
secrets with the all-knowing
Devourer."

1. Oþinn qvaþ:
"Raþ þv mer nv, Frigg! allz
mic fara tíðir
at vitia Vafðrvdnis; forvitni
micla
qveþ ec mer a fornom sta'fom
við þann inn alsvinna iotvn."

2. Frigg said:
"At home to stay
I would prefer the Host-Father
home in the settlements of the
gods;
for no Devourer, I have always
thought, was equally mighty/
cunning
as this Powerful Head Veil."

3. Óðinn said: "Much did I
travel much have I tried
much have I tested the powers; This will I know,
how the Powerful Head Veil
has cunningly made his hall."

4. Frigg said:
"May you fare whole! May you
return whole!
May you be whole on the path!
May your wisdom be enough
for you where you are going,
Father of Ages, to word-duel
with the Devourer!"

5. The Spirit traveled then to
contend in the word-duel
with the all-knowing Devourer; to the hall he came,
which Battle-Dust´s father
owned inside went The Terrible One[70] directly.

6. Óðinn said:
"Be whole, now, Powerful
Head-Veil now I have entered
the hall
to see your self;
and this is the first I wish to
know if you are wise
or all-knowing, Devourer."

2. Frigg qvaþ:
"Heima letia
ec munda Heriafaðr i garðom
goða; þviat engi iotvn
ec hvgða iafnramman sem
Vafðrvðni vera."

3. Oþinn qvaþ:
"Fiolþ ec fór, fiolþ ec freistaða,
fiaþ ec reynda regin; hitt vil
ec vita,
hve Vafðrvþnis salakynni se."

4. Frigg qvaþ:
'Heill þv farir! heill þv aptr
komir!
heill þv a sinnom sér! oþi þer
dvgi,
hvars þv scalt, Aldafaþr,
orðom meła iotvn!

5. For þa Oðinn at freista
orþspeci
þess ins alsvinna iotvns; at
haþlo hann com,
oc atti Íms faðir;
inn gecc Yggr þegar.

6. Oþinn qvaþ:
"Heill þv nv, Vafðrvðnir! nv
em ec i haþll kominn
a þic sialfan sia; hitt vil ec
fyrst vita, ef þv froþr ser
eþa alsviþr iotvnn."

7. Powerful Head-Veil said:
"Who is this human
who has entered my hall,
to whom am I giving words?
You will never come out of my halls alive
unless you are the wiser one."

8. Óðinn said:
"Wandering Counsel I am called now I have come walking thirsty to your hall
In need I am of your hospitality
-long have I traveled–
and of your welcome[71], Devourer!"

9. Powerful Head-Veil said:
"Why are you then, Wandering Counsel, speaking from the floor?
Take a seat in the hall! Then shall we test out which one is more wise
-the guest, or this ancient Reciting-Sage."

10. Óðinn said: "The poor man who comes to the wealthy should speak little or stay silent A great deal of too much speak,
I think, may be unfortunate for the one who visits The-One-Cold-From-Cunning."

11. Powerful Head-Veil said:
"Tell me then, Wandering Counsel, if from the hall-floor you want
to try your fortune; What is the horse called who always pulls
the Day to the ruling descendants [humans]?"

7. Vafþrvðnir qvaþ:
"Hvat er þat manna, er i mínom sal verpomc orði á?
vt þv ne comir orom hꜹllom ofra,
nema þv inn snotrari ser."

8.Oþinn qvaþ:
"Gagnraþr ec heiti,
nv emc af gongo kominn þyrstr til þinna sala, laðar þvrfi
— hefi ec lengi farit —
oc þinna andfanga, iotvnn!"

9.Vafþrvðnir qvaþ:
"Hvi þv þa, Gagnraþr, meliz af gólfi fyr? farþv i sess i sal!
þa scal freista, hvarr fleira viti,
gestr eþa inn gamli þulr."

10. Oþinn qvaþ:
"Oꜳþigr maþr, er til aꜳþigs kǫmr,
meli þarft eþa þegi; ofrmelgi micil
hygg ec, at illa geti hveím er viþ kaldrifiaðan kǫmr."

11. Vafþrvðnir qvaþ:
"Segþv mer, Gagnraþr, allz þv a gólfi vill
þins vm freista frama: hve sa hestr heitir,
er hverian dregr dag of drottmꜳgo?"

12. Óðinn said:
Shining Mane is he called
who draws Day to the rul-
ing descendants; the best of
horses
he is considered by the people
always gleams the mane of
this horse."

13. Powerful Head-Veil said:
"Tell me then, Wandering
Counsel, if from the hall-floor
you want
to try your fortune;
What is that steed called who
draws, from the East,
the Night to the beneficial
gods?"

14. Óðinn said:
"Frost-Fax he is called who
always draws
the Night to the beneficial
gods; From his bit he sheds
foam-drops, each morning,
from there comes the dew to
the valleys."

15. Powerful Head-Veil said:
"Tell me then, Wandering
Counsel, if from the hall-floor
you want
to try your fortune; What is
the river called, which divides
the Earth
between the sons of the Devourers and the gods?"

16. Óðinn said:
"Impetuosity is that river
called which divides the Earth
between
the sons of the Devourers and
the gods Freely she[72] shall flow
through the ages never shall
ice form upon her.

12. Oþinn qvaþ:
"Scinfaxi heitir, er inn scíra
dregr
dag vm drottmꞌgo;
hesta beztr þyccir hann meþ
Hreíðgotom,
ęy lysir maꞌn af mari."

13. Vafþrvðnir qvaþ:
"Segdv þat, Gagnraþr, allz þv
a gólfi vill
þins vm freista frama: hve sa
iór heitir,
er aꞌstan dregr nott of nyt
regin?"

14. Oþinn qvaþ:
"Hrímfaxi heitir, er hveria
dregr nott of nyt regin;
meldropa fellir hann morgin
hvern,
þaðan kǫmr daꞌgg vm dala."

15. Vafþrvðnir qvaþ:
Segðv þat, Gagnraþr, allz þv a
gólfi vill
þins vm freista frama: hve sv
á heitir,
er deilir meþ iotna sonom
grvnd oc meþ goðom?"

16. Oþinn qvaþ:
"Ifing heitir á,
er deilir meþ iotna sonom
grvnd oc meþ goðom; opin
renna
hon scal vm aldrdaga, verþrat
íss a á."

17. Powerful Head-Veil said:
"Tell me then, Wandering
Counsel, if from the hall-floor
you want
to try your fortune;
What is that battle-field called
where war shall find
the Sooted One and the sweet
gods?"[73]

18. Óðinn said:
"War-Surge is the field where
war shall find
the Sooted One and the sweet
gods; a hundred leagues
he stretches in each direction
this is the fated field."

19. Powerful Head-Veil said:
"You are wise, guest,
approach you the bench of
the Devourer and let us speak
together in the seat
we should wager our heads
in this hall, guest! On our
wisdom!"

17. Vafþrvðnir qvaþ:
"Segðv þat, Gagnraþr, allz þv
a gólfi vill
þins vm freista frama: hve sa
va͛llr heitir,
er finnaz vigi at
Svrtr oc in svaso goð?"

18. Oþinn qvaþ:
"Vigriþr heitir vollr, er finnaz
vigi at
Svrtr oc in svaso goð; hvndraþ
rasta
hann er a hverian veg, sa er
þeim vollr vitaþr."

19. Vafþrvðnir qvaþ:
"Froþr ertv nv gestr, far þv a
becc iotvns
oc melomc i sessi saman! ha͛fði
veðia
við scolom ha͛llo i, gestr! vm
geðspeki."

END OF ROUND ONE, IN THE WORD DUEL

ROUND TWO, IN THE WORD DUEL

20. Óðinn said: "Tell me the
first,
if your wit will do for you
and if you, Powerful Head-
Veil, knows: From where came
the Earth first,
or the heaven above, Oh, wise
Devourer?"

20. Oþinn qvaþ:
"Segðv þat iþ eína, ef þitt ǫþi
dvgir
oc þv, Vafþrvðnir, vitir:
hvaþan iorð vm com eþa vp-
phiminn
fyrst? inn froþi iotvnn!"

21. Powerful Head-Veil said:
"From the flesh of Sound was
the Earth created
and the mountains from his
bones,
Heaven from the skull
of the frost-cold Devourer
and from his blood the ocean."

22. Óðinn said: "Tell me the
second
if your wit will do for you
and if you, Powerful Head-
Veil, knows:
From where comes Moon he
who travels above people and
Sun the same?"

23. Powerful Head Veil said:
"Time-Traveler he is called he
is Moon´s father
and for Sun the same Through
heaven they must pass every
day
to count the years of the ages."

24. Óðinn said: "Tell me the
third
since you are known to be wise
and if you, Powerful Head-
Veil, knows: From where
comes the day,
who passes above mankind
and Night with her waxing
moonshine?"

25. Powerful Head-Veil said:
"Shining Famous One he is
called he is the father of Day
but Night was born of Slight
Death[74] Waxing and Waning
were made by the good powers
to count the years of the ages."

21. Vafþrvðnir qvaþ:
"Ór Ymis holdi
var iorð vm scarpvð, en or beinom biorg, himinn or harsi
ins hrimkalda iotvns, enn or
sveita sior."

22. Oþinn qvaþ:
"Segðv þat annat, ef þitt ęþi
dvgir
oc þv, Vafþrvðnir, vitir: hvadan máni kom,
sa er ferr menn yfir, eþa sol iþ
sama?"

23. Vafþrvðnir qvaþ:
"Mvndilfǫri heitir, hann er
Mána faþir oc sva Solar iþ
sama; himin hverfa
þar scolo hverian dag
aldom at ártali."

24. Oþinn qvaþ:
"Segðv þat iþ þriþia, allz
þic svinnan qveþa oc þv,
Vafþrvðnir, vitir: hvaðan dagr
vm com, sa er ferr drot yfir,
eþa nott meþ niðom?"

25. Vafþrvðnir qvaþ:
"Dellingr heitir, hann er Dags
faþir,
enn Nott var Narvi borin; ny
oc niþ
scopo nyt regin
aldom at artali."

26.Óðinn said: "Tell me the fourth
since you are known to be wise,
and if you, Powerful Head-Veil, knows: "From where came the winter first,
or the warm summer, among to the wise powers?"

27. Powerful Head-Veil said:
"Wind-Cool he is called
he is the father of Winter
but Mild Breeze fathered Summer;
... [text lost in manuscript]

28. Óðinn said: "Tell me the fifth
since you are known to be wise,
and if you, Powerful Head-Veil, knows:
Who is the oldest among the Aesir or among the descendants of Sound
who were born in the earliest times?"

29. Powerful Head-Veil said:
"Uncountable winters before Earth was created
then was Fruit-Bellower born
Power-Bellower was his father
and he was fathered by Rock-Matter-Bellower."

30. Óðinn said: "Tell me the sixth
since you are known to be wise,
and if you, Powerful Head-Veil, knows: From where came Rock-Matter-Bellower first
to be among the sons of the Devourers,
oh, wise Devourer!"

26. Oþinn qvaþ:
"Segðv þat iþ fiorþa, allz þic froþan qveþa, oc þv,
Vafþrvðnir, vitir: hvaðan vetr vm com eþa varmt svmar
fyrst meþ froþ regin?"

27. Vafþrvðnir qvaþ:
"Vindsvalr heitir, hann er Vetrar faþir, enn Svasvþr Svmars;
...

28.Oþinn qvaþ:
"Segdv þat iþ fimta, allz þic froþan qveþa, oc þv,
Vafþrvðnir, vitir: hverr asa ellztr
eþa Ymis niðia yrþi i ardaga?"

29. Vafþrvðnir qvaþ:
"Orófi vetra,
aþr veri iorþ vm scopvþ, þa var Bergelmir borinn;
Þrvdgelmir var þess faðir, enn Avrgelmir afi."

30. Oþinn qvaþ:
"Segðv þat it setta, allz þic svinnan qveþa,
oc þv, Vafþrvðnir, vitir: hvaþan Avrgelmir com meþ iotna sonom
fyrst? inn froþi iotvnn!"

31. Powerful Head-Veil said:
"From the Stormy Waves
dripped the poisonous drops
they grew until they became a
giant[Devourer];
From there have our lineages
all come together
this is why they are so destructive."

32. Óðinn said: "Tell me the
seventh
since you are known to be
wise,
and if you, Powerful Head-
Veil, knows: How did he beget
children,
that fierce Devourer,
if he never had pleasure with a
giantess?"

33. Powerful Head-Veil said:
"Beneath the frost giant´s
arms, it is said that they grew,
maiden and kinsman together;
one foot with the other foot
the wise Devourer begat a
six-headed son."

34. Óðinn said: "Tell me the
eight
since you are known to be
wise,
and if you, Powerful Head-
Veil, knows: What you first
remember,
or what you know to be the
earliest
-You are all-knowing, Devourer!"-

31. Vafþrvðnir qvaþ:
"Or Elivagom stvcco eítr-
dropar,
sva óx, vnnz or varð iotvnn;
þar ero órar ęttir
komnar allar saman,
því er þat ę allt til atalt."

32. Oþinn qvaþ:
"Segðv þat iþ siaunda, allz
þic svinnan qveþa, oc þv,
Vafþrvðnir, vitir: hve sa bǫrn
gat
enn balldni iotvnn, er hann
hafdit gygiar gaman?"

33. Vafþrvðnir qvaþ:
"Vndir hendi vaxa qvaþo
hrímþvrsi mey oc marg saman;
fótr við fǫti gat
ins froða iotvns sexharfðaþan
son."

34. Oþinn qvaþ:
"Segðv þat iþ átta, allz þic
froþan qveþa,
oc þv, Vafþrvðnir, vitir: hvat
þv fyrst vm mant eþa fremst
vm veitzt? þv ert alsviþr,
iotvnn."

35. Powerful Head-Veil said:
"Uncountable winters before
Earth was created
then was Fruit-Bellower born;
The first I remember
is when that wise Devourer
was first laid in his coffin."

36. Óðinn said: "Tell me the
ninth
since you are known to be
wise,
and if you, Powerful Head-
Veil, knows:
From where comes the wind
that passes across the waves
and which men never see in
itself?"

37. Powerful Head-Veil said:
"Corpse-Swallower he is called
who sits at the end of Heaven,
a Devourer in eagle´s hide;
From his wings
it is said that the wind begins
that passes across all men."[75]

38. Óðinn said: "Tell me the
tenth
since you are known to be
wise,
and if you, Powerful Head-
Veil, knows:
From where came Njǫrðr[76]
first to the sons of the Aesir
-temples and sanctuaries, he
rules over these -
even though he was raised
among Aesir."

35. Vafþrvðnir qvaþ:
"Orófi vetra,
aþr vęri iorð vm ska/pvð, þa
var Bergelmir borinn: þat ec
fyrst vm man,
er sa inn froþi iotvnn a var
lvðr vm lagiðr."

36. Oþinn qvaþ:
"Segðv þat iþ níunda, allz
þic svinnan qveþa, oc þv,
Vafþrvðnir, vitir: hvadan
vindr vm kǫmr, sva at ferr vág
yfir?
ę menn hann sialfan vm siá.

37. Vafþrvðnir qvaþ:
"Hręsvelgr heitir,
er sitr a himins enda, iotvnn i
arnar ham; af hans vengiom
qveþa vind koma alla menn
yfir."

38. Oþinn qvaþ:
"Segðv þat iþ tíunda, allz þu
tiva ra/c
a/ll, Vafðrvðnir, vitir: hvaðan
Niorðr vm kom
† meþ asa sonom?
— hofom oc ha/rgom hann
ręðr hvnnmorgom — oc
varþaþ hann asom alinn."

39. Powerful Head-Veil said:
"In the world of the Vanir
he was created by the wise
powers
and they sold him as a hostage
to the gods;
When the Age is shattered he
shall return back again
at home with the wise Vanir."

39. Vafþrvðnir qvaþ:
"I vanaheimi
scopo hann vis regin,
oc sęldo at gislingo goðvm; i
aldar rꜹc
hann mvn aptr coma
heim meþ visom vꜹnom."

40. Óðinn said:
"Tell me the eleventh;
In what courts do men fight
every day?"

40. Oþinn qvaþ:
"Segðv þat et ellipta: hvar ytar
tvnom i hꜹggvaz hverian dag?

41. Powerful Head-Veil said:
"All the Sole Rulers
on the fields of Spirit fight
every day;
They choose the slain and ride
from the battle
then they sit once more in
peace together."

41. Vafþrvðnir qvaþ:
"Allir einheriar Oðins tvnom i
hꜹggvaz hverian dag;
val þeir kiosa oc riþa vígi fra,
sitia meirr vm sáttir saman."

42. Óðinn said: "Tell me the
twelfth
since you are known to be
wise,
and if you, Powerful Head-
Veil, knows: Why do you,
Powerful Head-Veil, know all
the fate of the gods?
Of the secrets of Devourers
and of all the gods you speak
most truly, oh, all-knowing
giant!"

42. Oþinn qvaþ:
"Segþv þat iþ tolpta, hvi þv
tiva rꜹc
ꜹll, Vafðrvðnir, vitir? fra iotna
rv́ nom
oc allra goða
segir þv iþ sannasta, inn als-
vinni iotvnn!"

43. Powerful Head-Veil said:
"About the runes of the giants
and of all the gods
I can truly speak for I have
been to every world:
To nine worlds I came beneath
Misty Hel
where the dead come from
Hel´s halls.

43. Vafþrvðnir qvaþ:
"Fra iotna rv́ nom oc allra
goða
ec kann segia satt, þviat
hvern hefi ec heim vm komit:
nio kom ec heima, fyr niflhel
neðan,
hinig deyia or helio halir."

ROUND THREE, IN THE WORD DUEL

44. Óðinn said:
"Much have I traveled, much
have I tried much have I tested
the powers;
Which among men will survive
when the famed Mighty Winter comes among men?"

45. The Powerful Head-Veil
said:
"Life and Legacy-Tracker shall
both be hiding
within Treasure Memory´s
Holt The morning dew
they shall have for their nourishment and from them new
ages shall spring"

46. Óðinn said:
"Much have I traveled, much
have I tried much have I tested
the powers;
From where will the Sun come
into the smooth heaven
when Greed has quenched this
one?"

47. Powerful Head-Veil said:
"One daughter is born
to Elfin Splendor [the Sun
goddess] after she has been
quenched by Greed; She shall
ride when the Powers die the
maiden on her mother´s old
path."

48. Óðinn said:
"Much have I traveled, much
have I tried much have I tested
the powers;
Who are those maidens who
journey as one, so wise in their
spirit, across the ocean?"

44. Oþinn qvaþ:
"Fiolþ ec for, fiolþ ec
freistaþac,
fiolþ ec vm reynda regin: hvat
lifir manna,
þa er inn męra liþr fimbvlvetr
meþ firom?"

45. Vafþrvðnir qvaþ:
"Lif oc Leifþrasir, enn þaͬ
leynaz mvno i holti Hoddmim-
is; morgindͬggvar ðav ser at
mat hafa,
enn þaðan af aldir alaz."

46. Oþinn qvaþ:
"Fiolþ ec for, fiolþ ec
freistaþac,
fiolþ ec vm reynda regin:
hvaðan cǫmr sol
a inn sletta himin,
þa er þessa hefir Fenrir farit?"

47. Vafþrvðnir qvaþ:
"Eina dottvr berr Alfraͬðvll,
aþr hana Fenrir fari; sv scal
riða,
þa er regin deyia, modvr
braͬtir męr."

48. Oþinn qvaþ:
"Fiolþ ec for, fiolþ ec
freistaþac,
fiolþ ec vm reynda regin:
Hveriar 'ro þęr meyiar, ęr liþa
mar yfir, frodgediaþar fara?"

49. Powerful Head-Veil said:
"Three great tribal rivers run across the Earth
(they are) the Kin-Seeker´s maidens[fates]; They are hide-walkers/fortune-bringers who dwell in the world although they were raised among Devourers."[77]

50. Óðinn said:
"Much have I traveled, much have I tried much have I tested the powers;
Who among the Aesir will rule the realms of the gods when the fires of the Sooted One are quenched?"

51. Powerful Head-Veil said:
"Expanding Warrior and the Choice shall build the divine sanctuaries
when the fires of the Sooted One are quenched Power and Greatness
shall own the Grinder [Thor´s hammer] when Weapon-Quaker´s strife is over."[78]

52. Óðinn said:
"Much have I travelled, much have I tried much have I tested the powers;
What shall end the life of Spirit when the powers are torn asunder?"

49. Vafþrvðnir qvaþ:
"Þriar þioðár falla þorp yfir meyia Mꜹgþrasiss; hamingior einar þer er i heimi ero, þo þer meþ iotnom alaz."

50. Oþinn qvaþ:
"Fiolþ ec for, fiolþ ec freistaþac, fiolþ ec vm reynda regin: Hverir raþa ꜹsir eignom goða, þa er slocnar Svrta logi?"

51. Vafþrvðnir qvaþ:
"Viþarr oc Vali byggia vé goða, þa er slocnar Svrta logi; Móþi oc Magni scolo Miollni hafa Vingnis at vigþroti."

52. Oþinn qvaþ:
"Fiolþ ec for, fiolþ ec freistaþac, fiolþ ec vm reynda regin: hvat verþr Oðni at aldrlagi, þa er vm rivfaz regin?"

53. Powerful Head-Veil said:
"The Wolf [Greed] shall swallow the Father of Ages
that shall Expanding Warrior
avenge;
The cold yaws he shall cleave
through
thus quenching the Wit-
ness´ [Greed´s]war."

54. Óðinn said:
"Much have I travelled, much
have I tried much have I tested
the powers;
What did Spirit say
after he was laid on the pyre
into the ear of his own son
[Baldr]?"⁷⁹

55. Powerful Head-Veil: "No
man knows
what you in bygone days said
into the ear of your son. With
a mouth doomed to die
I spoke my ancient recitations
and about the Shattering of
the Rulers.
Now I have contended with
Spirit in a word-duel
you will always be the wisest."

53. Vafþrvðnir qvaþ:
"Vlfr gleypa mvn Aldafaꞃþr,
þess mvn Viþarr reca;
kalda kiapta hann klyfia mvn
vitnis vigi at."

54. Oþinn qvaþ:
"Fiolþ ec for, fiolþ ec
freistaþac,
fiolþ ec vm reynda regin: hvat
melti Oðinn,
aþr a bal stigi, sialfr i eyra
syni?"

55. Vafþrvðnir qvaþ:
"Ey manne þat veit, hvat þv
i ardaga sagdir i eyra syni;
feigom mvnni
melta ec mina forna stafi oc
vm ragnaraꞃc.
Nv ec viþ Oðin deildac mina
orþspeci,
þv ert e visastr vera."

GRIMNISMÁL

THE SPEECH OF THE MASKED ONE

In this poem, Óðinn and Frigg argue about the worthiness of their respective fosterlings, whom they raised. Frigg´s fosterling is Agnarr (Respect-Warrior) while Óðinn´s fosterling is Geirrǫðr (Red-Spear). Red-Spear betrays his brother in order to become sole king, and Respect-Warrior ends up living in a cave with a giantess. Óðinn teases Frigg for having a fosterling of no consequence, whereupon Frigg teases Óðinn for having a fosterling of no honor (being stingy to visitors). In order to prove his wife wrong, Óðinn travels to Red-Spear and is immediately captured and set between two fires. This is an important metaphor; Óðinn is, after all, the Spirit itself, the cosmic spirit, the human spirit, set between "two fires".

The two fires may represent the two lesser aspects of himself, the god being a trinity consisting of High, Equally High and the mysterious, transcendental Third (see the previous poem), or else consisting of Spirit and his two lesser brothers; Will and Awe, representing Intent/Desire and Thought/Mind. Red-Spear´s son, named after his uncle, Respect-Warrior, and thus a fusion between these two brothers, offers mead to Spirit and is rewarded with a great revelation about the world and about the true, all-encompassing, pantheistic nature of the great god of Spirit and Poetry.

Image from original printing of The Poetic Edda

ABOUT THE SONS OF KING CONFLICT- DESCENDANT.

Conflict-Descendant King had two sons, one called Respect-Warrior, and another called Red-Spear. Respect-Warrior was ten years old, and Red-Spear was eight. They both rowed out in a boat with a trailing line after small fish. The wind drove them out into the ocean.

In the dark night they wrecked on land, and went ashore, they found a place to stay for the winter. The old woman fostered Respect-Warrior, and the old man fostered Red-Spear. And when he and the old woman took them down to the shore, then the old man spoke privately to Red-Spear. They got a breeze and came to their father´s harbor.

Red-Spear was forward in the ship, he jumped ashore and pushed the ship back out and said: "Go where the trolls will take you!" The ship was driven out, and Red-Spear went up to the court. He was greeted joyfully, his father had died. Then Red-Spear was taken as king and became a splendid man.

Synir Hravdvngs konungs.

Hravdvngr konvngr atti tva sono, het annarr Agnarr, en annarr Geirraþr. Agnarr var tío vetra, enn Geirravdr átta vetra. Þeir rero tveir a bati með dorgar sinar at smafisci. Vindr rac þa i haf vt.

I natmyrkri brvto þeir við land oc gengo vp, fvndo cotbónda einn; þar voro þeir vm vetrinn. Kerling fostraþi Agnar, enn karl fostraþi Geirroð oc kendi hanom rað. At vári fecc karl þeim scip. Enn er þav kerling leiddo þa til strandar, þa melti karl einmeli við Geirravd.

Þeir fengo byr oc qvomo til stavdva farþvr sins. Geirroþr var fram i scipi; hann hlióp vp a land, enn hratt v́ t scipino oc melti: "Farþv nv þar er smyl hafi þic!"

Scipit rac i haf vt. Enn Geirroðr gek vpp til boiar, hanom var þar vel fagnat; enn faþir hans var þa andaþr. Var þa Geirravðr til konungs tekinn, oc varð maþr agetr.

Odin and Frigg sat in the Opening Shelf, looking into all the worlds. Odin said; "Do you see Respect-Warrior, your fosterling, there raising children with a giantess in a cave? But Red-Spear, my fosterling, is king and rules over the land.

Frigg says: "He is so stingy with food that he tortures his guests if it seems to him that too many have come." Odin says that this is a great lie. They wagered on the matter.

Frigg sent her handmaid, The Fulfilled One*, to Red-Spear. She told the king to beware lest a wizard, who had come into the country, should bewitch him, and said that he could be known by this sigh; that no dog was so fierce that it would attack him.

Oþinn oc Frigg sato i Hliþsciálfo oc sa vm heima alla. Odinn męlti: "Sér þv Agnar fostra þinn, hvar hann elr born við gygi i hellinom? Enn Geirroþr fostri minn er konungr oc sitr nv at landi."

Frigg segir: "Hann er maþniþingr sa, at hann qvelr gesti sina, ef hanom þiccia of margir coma." Oþinn segir, at þat er in mesta lygi; þa͛ vedia vm þetta mál. Frigg sendi escimey sína Fvllo til Geirroðar.

Hon bad konung varaz, at eigi fyrgerþi hanom fiolkvnnigr maþr sa er þar var kominn i land; oc sagdi þat marc á, at engi hvndr var sva olmr, at á hann mundi hla͛pa.

And it was the greatest slander that Red-Spear was not generous with food; however, he had the man whom no dog would attack arrested.

He was wearing a blue cloak and called himself Masked One, and would say nothing more about himself though he was asked.

The king had him tortured to make him speak and set him between two fires, and he sat there for eight nights.

Red-Spear King had a ten year old son, and he was named Respect-Warrior after his brother.

Respect-Warrior went to Masked One and gave him a horn filled with drink and said that it was bad what his father was doing, torturing a man without cause.

The Masked One drank from this, and then the fire had come so close that Masked One´s cloak was burning.

Enn þat var inn mesti hegomi, at Geirroþr konungr veri eigi matgoþr; oc þo letr hann handtaca þann mann, er eigi vildo hvndar a ráða. Sa var i feldi blám oc nefndiz Grimnir og sagði ecci fleíra fra ser, þott hann veri at spvrþr. Konvngr let hann pína til sagna oc setia milli elda tveggia, oc sat hann þar átta netr.

Geirroþr konvngr atti þa son tío vetra gamlan, oc het Agnarr eptir broþur hans.

Agnarr gecc at Grimni oc gaf hanom horn fvlt at drecca oc sagði, at faðir hans gorði illa, er hann píndi þenna mann sacla⁄san. Grimnir dracc af; þa var eldrinn sva kominn, at feldrinn brann af Grimni.

Depiction of Odin on Slepnir with horn in hand-Public Domain

He spoke:

1. "Hot are you, fire, and rather
too fierce away with you, sparks
my fur cloak singes
though I lift it up in the air
my mantle shall burn before me

2. Eight nights did I sit between
the fire here so that many to me
refused to offer nourishment

Only Respect-Warrior who shall
rule alone Red-Spear´s son
over the lands of the Goths

3. Whole you shall be, Respect-Warrior! Since the God of
Being[80] bids you to stay whole.
For one drink you shall never
have a better reward.

THE TWELVE WORLDS

4. The land is holy that I see
lying
close to the elves and to the Aesir gods and in the Power World
there shall Thor [Thunder]
stay until the powers are torn
asunder

5. Yew-valleys it is called, where
Ullr[81] has made a hall for himself
The World of Elves
was given to Freyr [fertility,
civilization] in bygone days, as a
tooth-gift.

6. There is a third home where
the kindly powers roofed the hall
with silver
The Shelf of Choice it is called
which the god made for himself
in bygone days.

Hann qvaþ:

1. Heitr ertv, hripvþr! oc heldr til
micill; gongomc firr, fvni! loði
sviþnar,
þott ec a lopt berac, brennomc
feldr fyr.

2. Átta nętr sat ec milli elda her,
sva at mer mangi mat ne barð ,
nema einn Agnarr, er einn scal
ráða, Geirroþar sonr, Gotna
lande.

3. Heill scaltv, Agnarr! allz þic
heilan biþr Veratyr vera;
eins drycciar þv scalt aldregi
betri giold geta.

4. Land er heilact, er ec liggia
se asom oc alfom nęr; enn i
Þrvðheimi scal Þórr vera,
vnz vm rivfaz regin.

5. Ydalir heita þar er Vllr hefir
ser vm gorva sali; Alfheim Freý
gáfo i ardaga tivar at tannfę.

6. Bor er sa inn þriði er blið regin
silfri þarcþo sali; Valascialf heitir,
er vęlti ser
áss i ardaga.

7. Sunken River is a fourth world
called and cool waves resound
above it
There Poetry [Óðinn] and History[82] drink together every day
happily from golden goblets

8. Happy World a fifth world is
called There gold-bright Valhalla
rises peacefully, seen from afar
There the Shattered One[83]
chooses every day those who
died by weapons

9. Exceedingly easy it is to
recognize for those who come
to Spirit [Óðinn]: to see how his
hall is arranged;
Spear-shafts for rafters with
shields it is thatched
mail-coats are strewn on the
benches.

10. Exceedingly easy it is to
recognize for those who come
to Poetry [Óðinn] to see how his
hall is arranged:
A wolf [Greed/Desire] hangs in
front of the western door
and an eagle [Death] hovers
above.

11. The World of Drumming a
sixth is called where Slave-Binder [Death][84] dwells
the almighty Devourer
and now Harm[85] is building that
shining bride of the gods
living in her father´s ancient
courts

7. Saᴗcqvabeccr heitir enn fiorþi,
enn þar svalar knego
vnnir yfir glymia;
þar þaᴗ Oðinn oc Sága drecca
vm alla daga glaᴗð or gvllnom
kerom.

8. Glaðsheimr heitir enn fimti,
þars en gvllbiarta
Valhaᴗll við of þrvmir;
enn þar Hroptr kýss
hverian dag vapndaᴗþa vera.

9. Mioc er aᴗþkent þeim er til
Oþins koma, salkynni at sia;
scaᴗptom er rann rept,
scioldom er salr þakiþr, bryniom
vm becki strát.

10. Mioc er aᴗþkent þeim er til
Oþins koma, salkynni at sia;
vargr hangir fyr vestan dyrr
oc drvpir aᴗrn yfir.

11. Þrymheimr heitir enn setti, er
Þiazi bió
sa inn amátki iotvnn; enn nv
Scaði byggvir, scír brvðr goða,
fornar toptir faᴗðvr.

12. Broad View is the seventh world and there Baldr [Courage] has
built a hall for himself in this land
I know there lies the fewest evil plots

13. Mountain of Heaven is the eight world and there Great World[86]
rules the sanctuaries
there the glad watchman of the gods
drinks the good mead in his comfortable hall.

14. People Field is the ninth world And there Freyia [Fate] rules
the seating of the hall[87] half of the chosen
she chooses every day
the other half owns Óðinn.

15. Glittering is the tenth world and he is buttressed with gold
and silver-roofed the ceiling there, Front-Seat [Justice]
builds, most of the days
and quenches every quarrel

16. Ship´s Harbor is the eleventh world and there Njǫrðr [Winds and Waves]owns a hall made for himself
that prince of men lacking in malice
rules the high-timbered temple

17.   Brushood grows and high grass
widely in the lands of the Expanding Wood[88] and there the son proclaims
at the back of a mare
that he is keen to avenge his father

12. Breiðablik ero in siavndo, enn þar Baldr hefir
ser vm gerva sali; a þvi landi
er ec liggia veit fǫsta feícnstafi.

13. Himinbiorg ero en atto, enn þar Heimdall
qveþa valda veom; þar vorþr
goða dreccr i vęro ranni glaþr
inn góða mioþ.

14. Folcvangr er inn nivndi, enn þar Freyia ręþr sessa costom
i sal; halfan val
hon kyss hverian dag, enn halfan Oðinn á.

15. Glitnir er inn tivndi, hann er gvlli stvddr
oc silfri þacþr iþ sama; enn þar Forseti byggir flestan dag
oc svęfer allar sacir.

16. Nóatvn ero en ellipto, enn þar Niorþr hefir
ser vm gorva sali; manna þengill enn meinsvani
hatimbroþom ha˞rgi ręðr.

17. Hrísi vex oc há grasi Viðars land Viði;
en þar mavgr of lęzc af mars baki
frǫcn at hefna fa˞þvr.

VALHALLA

18. Spirit-Burner lets Fire-Burn-
er[89]
cook in Sea-Burner the best of
meat But few know
what the Sole Rulers (really) eat.

18. Andhrimnir lętr i Eldhrimne
Sęhrimni sodinn: flesca bezt,
enn þat fáir vito,
við hvat einheriar alaz.

19. To Act and To Desire[90] tamed
to war, are sated
by the conflicting Father of Rulers but on wine alone
the weapon-fair Spirit always
lives

19. Gera oc Freca seðr gvnntam-
iþr hroþigr Heriafaðr; enn viþ
vín eitt vapngafvgr
Oðinn ę lifir.

20. The Thought and The Memory fly every day
across the world so widely
I fear for Thought that he may
not return but I fear more for
Memory

20. Hvginn oc Mvninn flivga
hverian dag iormvngrvnd yfir;
ovmc ec of Hvgin,
at hann aptr ne comiþ,
þo siámc meirr vm Mvnin.

21. Thin-Mist roars
the fish of People-Witness[91]
swims in the stream
the river´s current seems very
hard to wade for those who
rejoice in slaughter[92]

21. Þytr þvnd, vnir þióþvitnis fis-
cr floði í; árstramr þickir ofmicill
Valglamni at vaþa

22. The Gate of Choice it is
called standing on the plain
holy before holy doors Ancient is
that gate but few know
how it is closed up with a lock

22. Valgrind heitir, er stendr velli
á
heilog fyr helgom dvrom; forn er
sv grind,
enn þat fáir vito,
hve hon er i lás vm lokin.

23. Five hundred doors and
forty more
I think there are in the Hall of
Choice:
Eight hundred Sole Rulers walk
as one through the door when
they move to fight
the Witness [The wolf of Greed]

23. Fimm hvndrvþ dvra oc vm
fiorom togom,
sva hygg ec á Valhallo vera; átta
hvndrvþ eínheria
ganga senn or einom dvrom, þa
er þeir fara við vitni at vega.

24. Five hundred floors and forty more
I think there are in Diminishing Shine
Of all those halls which I know
to be roofed my son´s, I think, is the greatest.[93]

24. Fimm hvndrvþ golfa oc vm fiorom togom,
sva hygg ec Bilscirni meþ bvgom;
ranna þeirra, er ec rept vita,
míns veit ec mest magar.

25. Bright Open Space Symbol is the she-goat called who stands above the hall
of the Father of Rulers
and bites off the limbs of the Wind-Shielded Counsel She will fill a vat of shining mead (of immortality) that drink can never diminish[94]

25. Heiþrv́ n heitir geit, er stendr hɑllo a † Heriafɑdrs
oc bitr af Lęraþs limom; scapker fylla hon scal ins scíra miaðar,
knaat sv veig vanaz.

26. Oak-Antlers is the stag´s name Who stands on the hall of the Father of Rulers and from his horns liquid
drips into the Resounding Mill [of Death][95]
from where all the rivers flow:

26. Eikþyrnir heitir hiortr, er stendr a hɑllo † Heriafɑþrs
oc bítr af Lęraþs limom; enn af hans hornom drypr i Hvergelmi,
þaðan eigo votn ɑll vega.

LISTING THE COSMIC "RIVERS"

27. Slow and Wide, Forward-Pushing and Fury, Cool and Battle-Seeking
Hurrying and Great Reciting Sage Rhine and Running
Gaping and Glaring
Ancient and Spear-Bubbling
These rivers flow round the realms of the gods: Roaring and Man-Friend, Tholl and
Hall Greed and Battle-Eager

27. Siþ oc Víþ, Sękin oc Ękin, Svɑl oc Gvnnþró, Fiorm oc Fim-bvlþvl, Rín oc Rennandi,
Gipvl oc Gɑpvl, Gɑmvl oc Geir-vimvl,
þęr hverfa vm hodd goða; Þyn oc Vin, Þɑll oc Hɑll, Graþ oc Gvnnþorin.

28. Woman-Friend is one´s name, another Distance-Diminisher [=Traveler] A third is Tribe-Devourer
Useful and Stinging, Strength and Wave Dangerously-Sharp and Stormy, Devourer and She-Wolf
Plight and Hope, Difficult and Shore Bellowing and Lightning, they flow close to men
and flow down from here to Hel [Death]

28. Vína heitir enn, annor Vegsvinn,
þriðia Þiodnvma; Nyt oc Navt,
Nann oc Hravnn, Sliþ oc Hríþ,
Sylgr oc Ylgr,
Víþ oc Ván, Vand oc Strand,
Giall oc Leiptr,
þer falla gvmnom nęr, en falla til heliar heðan.

29. Protection and Diverting and the two Kettle-Baths:
these must Thor wade every day when he goes to sit as judge
by the ash Yggdrasill
for the bridge of the Aesir burns all with flames
the sacred waters boil.

29. Kavrmt oc Avrmt oc Kerlavgar tvęr,
þer scal Þorr vaða dag hvern, er hann dǫma ferr
at asci Yggdrasils; þviat asbrv brenn all loga, heilog votn hlóa.

THE STEEDS OF THE AESIR

30. Glad and Golden, Glassy and Contest-Winning
Silver mane and Sinewy Brilliant and Hidden-Hoof Goldmane and Light-Foot
These horses the Aesir ride every day when they go to sit as judges by the ash Yggdrasill[96]

30. Glaþr oc Gyllir, Gler oc Sceiðbrimir, Silfrintoppr oc Sinir,
Gísl oc Falhofnir, Gvlltoppr oc Lettfeti,
þeim ríða ęsir ióm dag hvern, er þeir dǫma fara
at asci Yggdrasils.

THE WORLD TREE

31. Three roots stand growing in three directions
beneath the ash Yggdrasill
Hel [Death] lives beneath one
Frost-giants beneath another
beneath the third, human men

31.Þriár rǫtr standa a þria vega vndan asci Yggdrasils: Hel býr vnd einni, annarri hrimþvrsar,
þriðio mennzkir menn.

32. Wandering Pouch is the squirrel that must run
upon the ash Yggdrasill words of the Eagle [Death] he must often carry
and tell the Shame Biter below

33. There are harts, four of them gnawing (at the ash)
with their necks outstretched Dying and Hibernation
Downy-Ears and Slumber-Faith

34. There are more vipers lying beneath the ash Yggdrasill
than an ignorant ape may imagine In-the-Ground and On-the-Heath They are Grave-Witness´ sons Grey-Back and Grave-Fields Opener and Closer
I believe, that they forever will bite on the tree´s branches

35. The Ash Yggdrasill suffers in agony
more than men may know a stag bites from above
it decays on the sides
and Shame-Biter eats from beneath

36. Quaking and Misty
I want them to carry the drinking horn to me Axe-Age and Battle
Combat and Power
Battle-Noise and Army-Fetters Outcry and Spear-Charge
Shield-Truce and Council-Truce and Ruling Legacy;
They carry ale to the Sole Rulers[97]

32. Ratatoscr heitir ikorni, er renna scal
at asci Yggdrasils: arnar orð
hann scal ofan bera
oc segia Níþhꜹggvi niþr

33. Hirtir ero oc fiorir, þeirs af hꜹfingar á gaghalsir gnaga:
Dainn oc Dvalinn, Dvneyrr oc Dvraþrór.

34. Ormar fleiri liggia vnd asci Yggdrasils,
enn þat vf hyggi hverr osviþra apa:
Goinn oc Moinn,
þeir 'ro Grafvitnis synir, Grabacr oc Grafvꜹllvþr, Ofnir oc Svafnir,
hygg ec, at ę scyli meiþs qvisto má.

35. Ascr Yggdrasils drygir erfiði meira en menn vm viti: hiortr bítr ofan,
enn a hliþo fv́ nar, scerþer Níðhꜹggr neþan.

36. Hrist oc Mist
vil ec at mer horn beri, Sceggiꜹld oc Scꜹgvl, Hildr oc Þrvðr,
Hlꜹcc oc Herfiotur, Gꜹll oc Geirꜹnvl, Randgriþ oc Raþgriþ oc Reginlęif;
þęr bera einheriom ꜹl.

37. Early-Awake and All-White
these must always pull upwards,
wearily, the Sun from here;
but beneath their bellies good
powers disguised
a cooling stemming from iron[98]

38. Cool-One he is called who
stands before the Sun
a shield before the shining deity[99] Mountains and seas
I know would surely burn if he
falls from his post

39. Mockery is that wolf called
who follows the shine-skinned
deity to the protecting woods
Hatred is another one,
he is the son of Rage-Witness
who chases the bright bride of
Heaven.[100]

40. From the flesh of Sound was
the Earth created
and from the blood; the sea
mountains from the bones trees
from the hair
and from the skull; Heaven.

41. And from his eyelashes the
cheerful powers made
Middle World for the children of
men and from his brain
were made all the hard-tem-
pered clouds

37. Arvacr oc Alsviþr þeir scolo
vpp heðan svangir sol draga; enn
vnd þeirra bógom fálo bliþ regin,
ęsir, isarn kol.

38. Svalinn heitir, hann stendr
solo fyr, scioldr, scinanda goði;
biorg oc brim
ec veit at brenna scolo, ef hann
fellr ifrá.

39. Scᴧll heitir vlfr,
er fylgir eno scírleita goði til
varna viðar;
enn annarr Hati,
hann er Hroþvitnis sonr,
sa scal fyr heiða brvði himins

40. Ór Ymis holdi var iorþ vm
scᴧpvð, enn or sveita sær, biorg
or beinom, baðmr or hári,
en or hᴧsi himinn.

41. Enn or hans brám gerðo blið
regin Miðgard manna sonom;
enn or hans heila
varo þᴧ in harðmoðgo
scy ᴧll vm scᴧpvþ.

INVOCATION

42. May he have the protection
of Ullr and of all the gods
whoever first quenches the
flames
for the world lies open for the
sons of gods when they lift off
the kettles!

42. Vllar hylli hefr oc allra goða
hverr er tecr fyrstr a fvna; þviat
opnir heimar
verþa vm ása sonom, þa er hefia
af hvera.

43. The sons of the Inner Ruler
set out, in times bygone
to create Woodchips the best of
ships
for shining Freyr they made it,
for that benevolent child of
Njǫrðr [= wind and waves].[101]

43. Ivalda synir gengo i ardaga
Sciþbladni at scapa, scipa bezt,
scirom Frey, nytom Niarðar bvr.

44. The ash Yggdrasill is the best
among trees
Woodchips the foremost among
ships Spirit [Óðinn] among the
Aesir
Gliding-One [Sleipnir][102] among
horses Shivering-Voice among
bridges
Bragi among poets
High-Hose among hawks
and among dogs, Gluttony is
foremost

44. Ascr Yggdrasils hann er ǫztr
viþa,
en Sciþblaþnir scipa, Odinn asa,
enn ioa Sleipnir, Bilraͬst brv́ a,
en Bragi scalda,
Habroc haͬca, en hvnda Garmr.

45. I have now revealed my face
Among the sons of victorious
gods[103]
Now shall that desired nourishment wake:
I shall bring in all the Aesir to
the benches of Aegir
at the drinking- banquet of
Aegir.[104]

45. Svipom hefi ec nv ypt fyr
sigtiva sonom,
viþ þat scal vilbiorg vaca;
aͬllom asom
þat scal inn coma Ęgis becci á,
Ægis drecco at.

Revelation [Óðinn´s names]

46. I called myself Masked
I called myself Wandering
Learning The Ruler, the Hel-
met-Carrier [=Carrier of the
Mind]
Beloved and Third Thin Mist
and Wave
Death-Blinder and High

46. Hetomc Grímr, hetomc Gangleri, Herian oc Hialmberi, Þeccr
oc Þriði, Þuðr oc Uðr, Helblindi
oc Hár.

47. Truth and Perishable and Truth-Guesser Joy of the Moment and Pushing Forth Towards Sight, Fire-Eyed Harm-Doer, **The One Who Is Many**
Hooded and Masked
Bright Knowledge and Much Knowing

48. Broad Hat, Broad Beard Victory Father and Pushed All Father, Choice Father
Close Weight and God of Burdens
Never did I have just one name as I moved among people

49. I was called The Masked One in the halls of Spear Source and Castrate in the house of Divine Origin Cauldron I was called when I pulled the sledge Faith at the parliament Expander at the battleground Wish and Resounding Just-as-High and Shivering Calm Magic Wand and Long-Beard among the gods

50. The Burner and the Burned I was called at Sunken Memory I tricked the ancient giant when the son of Mead-Witness the mighty giant died in battle with me

51. Drunken are you, Red-Spear! you have drunk too much you lose much when you lose my favor and that of all the Sole Rulers.

47. Saðr oc Svipall oc Sanngetall, Herteitr oc Hnicarr, Bíleygr, Báleygr, Bólvercr, Fiölnir, Grímr oc Grímnir, Glapsviðr oc Fiölsviðr

48. Siþhattr, Siþsceggr, Sigfaðr, Hnicuðr, Alfaðr, Valfaðr, Atríðr oc Farmatyr; eino nafni hetomc aldregi, siz ec meþ folcom fór

49. Grimne mic héto at Geir-raðar, enn Ialc at Asmundar, enn þa Kialar er ec kialca dró, Þrór þingom at, Viðvrr at vigom, Osci oc Ómi, Iafnhár oc Biflindi, Göndlir oc Hárbarðr meþ goðom

50. Sviðurr oc Sviðrir er ec het at Söccmimis, oc dulða ec þann inn aldna iotun, þa er ec Miðviþnis varc ins mora bvrar ordinn einbani.

51. Avlr ertv, Geirroþr! hefr þv ofdrvccit, miclo ertv hnvgginn, er þv ert mino gengi, ollom ein-heriom

52. Much did I tell you and little you recall
your friend has deceived you
I see the sword of my friend
lying all covered in blood

52. Fiolþ ec þer sagðac, enn þv fatt vm mant,
of þic vela vinir; męki liggia
ec se mins vinar allan i dreyra drifinn.

53. The Chosen who are tired of sword-edges The Old/Terrible One[105] wants to have now
I know that your life has passed
the goddesses are against you[106]
now you may see The Spirit;
Draw near to me, if you are able!

53. Ęggmoþan val nv mvn Yggr hafa,
þitt veit ec líf vm liþit; v́ var 'ro disir,
nv knattv Oðin siá;
nalgaztv mic, ef þv megir!

54. The Spirit, the name is now The Old One I was before
and Thin Mist before that
Awakening and Shivering Veiled Wave and Shattered God Human and Castrate among gods Opener and Closer
and all I believe stem from me only.

54. Óðinn ec nu heiti, Yggr ec áþan het, hetvmc Þundr fyrir þat: Vacr oc Scilfingr, Váfuþr oc Hroptatýr,
Gautr oc Ialcr meþ goðom, Ofnir oc Svafnir,
er ec hygg at orðnir se allir af einom mer.

GRǪTTASǪNGR

THE SONG OF THE MILL-STONE OF DESTINY

A poem of the 13th century collection of Old Norse mythological poems known as "Edda Poetry". The poem has been transmitted to us from Snorri Sturluson´s "Skaldskaparmál" (The Speech About the Making of Poetry) where it is recited as a way of understanding poetic metaphors for "Gold". The two giant maidens in this poem are associated with the almighty giantesses who appear in the Vǫluspá stanza 8, prompting the gods into creating the dwarfs (images of men) and then human beings, upon which the giantesses appear again as norns creating the laws of destiny, and later again as valkyriur who choose the fallen in battle.

In this poem, the ladies appear in all three ways – firstly they instigate movement from within the depths of Earth, secondly they grind fate, thirdly they instigate wars before they are taken "prisoners" by "Wisdom" and made to grind prosperity to his realm – until they are fed up with his sleeping blindness and endless greed and grind the apocalypse into being...

The engraving shows the giantesses Fenja and Menja beside the mill Grótti. One giantess is sitting near the center of the frame while the other is standing by the side. In the bottom right corner there is the signature of Carl Larsson (1853-1919), the artist and a date of [18]86. In the bottom left corner there is the signature of Gunnar Forssell (1859-1903), the xylographer. The image list on page 468 in the book describes this image as "Fenja och Menja vid kvarnen Grotte".

The Song of the Mill Stone-Stone of Destiny

Why is gold called the Flour of Wisdom? To answer that the story goes thus....

Odin´s son was called Shield, and from him are the Skioldunga lineage descended; he had his seat and ruled the lands that are now known as Denmark, but which was then called Gotland. Shield had that son who was called Peace Heritage, and he ruled the lands after him. The son of Peace Heritage was called Wisdom, he took the kingdom after his father, in that time when Augustus Caesar ruled and there was peace in all lands, then was Christ born.

And because of Wisdom being the mightiest King in the Northern lands, so the peace was known by him in all Danish tongues, and the North-men called that age the Peace of Wisdom. No man would hurt another, even if he saw the bane of his father or the bane of his brothers free or even bound; there were no thieves and no robbers, to the point where a golden ring lay a long time on the Ialangr-Heath.

King Wisdom sought a visit to Sweden to that king who is named Many-One/Very Much [Odin], and from him he bought two she-slaves whose names were Heath-Dweller and Necklace Wearer (or Achiever and Rememberer); they were large and strong.

Hví er gull kallat Mjöl Fróða?
Til þess er saga sjá…

Skioldr het sonr Oþins, er Skioldvngar erv fra komnir; hann hafþi atsetv oc reð londvm, þar sem nv er kavllvt Danma/rk, en þa var kallat Gotland. Skioldr atti þann son, er Friþleifr het, er lond- vm reð eptir hann. Sonr Frilleifs het Froþi, hann toc konungdom eptir favþvr sinn, i þann tið er Avgvstvs keisari lagþi frið of heim allan; þa var Kristr borinn.
En firir þvi at Froþi var allra konunga rikastr a nordrlondvm, þa var hon- vm kendr friþrinn vm alla danska tungv, oc kalla Norðmenn þat Froþa Frið.

Engi maðr grandaþi avðrvm, þott hann hitti firir ser foþvrbana eþa broþvrbana lavsan eþa bvndinn; þa var oc engi þiofr eþa ransmaðr, sva at gvllhringr einn la a Ialangrsheiðe lengi. Froþi konungr sotti heimboð i Sviðioð til þess konungs er Fiolnir er nefndr, þa keypti hann ambattir tvær, er hetv Fenia oc Menia; þær vorv miklar oc sterkar.

In that time there was in Denmark a mill- stone so very big, that no man was so strong that he could pull it, and in the nature of this mill-stone it was so that it would grind what the miller spoke.

This mill-stone´s name was Grotti; Hanging Open Mouth he is called, who gave the mill-stone to King Wisdom. King Wisdom led the slave-girls to the mill- stone and asked them to grind gold and peace in the service of Wisdom.

Then he gave the women no more rest and no more sleep than the time it takes for a cuckoo to keep silent, or the time needed to speak forth a verse.

It is said that the women then sang a song that is called the Grotti-song:

I þann tima fannz i Danmork kvernsteinar tveir sva miklir, at engi var sva sterkr, at dregit giæti; en sv nattvra fylgþi kvernvnvm, at þat molz a kverninni, sem sa mælti firir er mol.

Sv kvern het Grotti; Hengikioptr er sa nefndr, er Froþa konungi gaf kvernina. Froði konungr let leiþa ambattirnar til kvernarinnar oc bað þær mala gvll oc friþ oc sælv Froþa.

Þa gaf hann þeim eigi lengri hvild eþa svefn, en ga/ krinn þagþi eþa hlioð matti qveþa.

Þa er sagt, at þær qvæþi lioð þav er kallat er Grottasavngr,

---

1. Now there have come to the house of the king two prescient women:
Heath-Dweller/Achiever
and Necklace-Owner/Rememberer:
They were with Wisdom, Son of Peace-Heritage:
The Mighty Maidens
he owned as his slave-girls.

1. Nv erv komnar til konvngs hvsa framvisar tvær:
Fenia
oc Menia;
þær 'ro at Froþa Friþleifs sonar Máttkar Meyiar at mani hafþar.

2. (The slave-girls) were led to the mill where they ordered
the gray stones
to grind into motion
He promised them neither rest nor pleasure
until he had heard the slave-girls´ song.

2. Þær at lvðri leiddar vorv oc griotz gria
gangs of beiddv; het hann hvarigri hvild ne yndi,
aðr hann heyrþi hliom ambatta.

3. They kept up the sound of the never-silent mill
"Let us set down the grinder let us stop the millstones!"
But he bid the Maidens to keep grinding as they owed.

4. They sang and they turned the fast-revolving stone
so that the Household of Wisdom mostly fell asleep
Then sang the Necklace-Owner/Rememberer who had come to the milling:

5. "Let us grind prosperity for Wisdom let us grind joyfully abundance of everything on the mill of fortune Let him sit on gold
Let him sleep on feathers Let him wake to happiness That is well ground out.

6. Here shall no one bring harm to another not plot damage
or strive to take lives Nor shall he strike with a sharp sword even if he finds bound the bane of his brother."

7. He did not speak at all except these few words: "You shall not sleep
any longer than the hall´s cuckoo or longer than I take to recite a verse."

3. Þær þyt þvlv þagnhorvinnar:
«leggivm lvðra, lettvm steinvm»;
bað hann enn Meyiar, at þær mala skyldv.

4. Svngv oc slvngv snvðga steini,
sva at Froþa man flest sofnaþi;
þa qvað þat Menia, var til meldrar komin:

5. Avð molvm Froþa, molvm alsælan, fiolð fiar
a feginslvðri; siti hann á avþi,
sofi hann a dvni,
vaki hann at vilia, þa er vel malit.

6. Her skyli engi aðrvm granda, til bals bva
ne til bana orka ne havggva þvi hvossv sverþi,
þo at bana broþvr bvndinn finni.»

7. En hann qvað ecki orð it fyrra:
«Sofit eigi þit ne of sal gavkar
eþa lengr en sva lioð eitt qveþac.»

8. (The Maidens sing:)
"Beware, Wisdom you are not
fully wise
you friend of human elo-
quence when you bought the
slave girls and chose them for
their strength and for their
appearance
but of their lineage you asked
not...

9. Hard was the Roaring One
and his father
although the Slave-Binder[107]
was mightier still
The Moving One and
Earth-Dweller our close kinsmen
brothers of mountain giants:
From them are we two born!

10. The Mill of Fate would not
have fallen
from the grey mountains,
nor would the hard stone
block have come out of the
Earth, nor would we have
ground so
-we rock giant maidens if we
had not known
how she[108] was made.

11. We grew nine winters we
were playful[109] great maidens
growing
nourished beneath the Earth:
We Maidens where the direc-
tors of great deeds:
All by ourselves we moved
the flat mountain from its
place.

8. «Varattv, Froþi! fvllspakr
of þic, malvinr manna! er þv
man keyptir; ka/ssþv at afli
oc at alitvm, en at ætterni ecki
spvrþir.

9. Harðr var Hrvngnir oc hans
faþir,
þo var Þiazi þeim a/flgari, Iþi
oc Avrnir okrir niðiar, bræðr
bergrisa,
þeim ervm bornar!'

10. Komia Grotti or gria fialli
ne sa hinn harþi hallr or Iorþv,
ne moli sva mær bergrisa, ef
vissi vitt
vetr til hennar.

11. Vær vetr niv vorvm leikvr
avflgar alnar firir iorð neþan;
stoþv Meyiar
at meginverkvm, færþvm sial-
far setberg or stað.

12. We rolled the boulder (the Mill/ Earth) from the world of the giants
so that the Earth began to shake we turned then
the fast-revolving stone (the Mill/ Earth) to the high hall
so that men took it.

12. Velltvm grioti of garð risa,
sva at fold firir for skialfandi;
sva slongþvm vit snvðga steini,
hofga halli,
at halir tocv.

13. But later we
in the land of the Swedes
-we two who know fate: moved among people
We broke armors
and we broke shields:
We marched against the gray-clad armies.

13. En vit siþan a Sviðioþv
-framvisar tvær i folk stigvm;
sneiddvm brynivr, en brvtvm skioldv;
gengvm i gegnvm graserkiat lit.

14. We overthrew some supported others we gave good help
to the people of Divine Serpent There was no peace until Knuckles fell

14. Steyptvm stilli, stvddvm annan, veittvm goþvm Gothormi lið, vara kyrrseta,
aðr Knvi felli.

15. We kept going for some seasons
so that we became famous for our battle deeds;
there we sliced with sharp spears blood from wounds made swords red.

15. Framm heldvm þvi þav misseri,
at við ad ka/ppvm kenndar vorvm; þar skorþv vit ska/rpvm geirvm bloð or benivm oc brand vm.

16. Now we have come
to the house of the king without compassion towards slave-girls mud eats at our feet
and we are otherwise chilled we pull the Calmer of Strife but there is no joy at Wisdom´s house

16. Nv ervm komnar til konvngs hvsa miskvnnlavsar
oc at mani hafþar; avrr etr iliar,
en ofan kvlði, drogvm dolgs siotvl, daprt er at Froþa.

17. Hands should rest
Let the stone stand still I have
ground
my full share;
We may not to our hands give
rest
until fully ground as Wisdom
sees it.

18. Hands shall clasp the hard
shafts
weapons bloodstained...
Wake you, Wisdom! Wake
you, Wisdom! If you wish to
hear our songs
and ancient tales.

19. I see a fire burn east of the
city
a war-spell has woken that
must be a beacon; an army
will come here very soon
and burn the settlement
despite the Abundance-De-
scendant (Wisdom).

20. You shall not keep
the throne of Lejre (Denmark)
nor the red-gold rings
nor this Ruling Rock (=the
millstone of fate) Let us seize
the handle:
Maiden! Turn (the Mill) more
swiftly!
We are not yet warmed by the
death-stir (=blood)

21. My father´s maiden
ground powerfully
so that she foresaw the death
of multitudes
the great shafts snapped away
from the Mill´s frame en-
closed in iron,
Let us grind even more

17. Hendr skolo hvilaz, hallr
standa mvn, malit hefi ec firir
mic mitt of leiti;
nv mvna hondvm hvild vel
gefa, aðr fvllmalit Froþa þycki.

18. Hendr skolo hølða harðar
trionor, vapn valdreyrvg,
vaki þv Froþi! vaki þv Froþi! ef
þv hlyþa vill songvm ockrvm
oc sa/gvm fornvm

19. Eld se ec brenna firir
avstan borg, vigspioll vaka,
þat mvn viti kallaðr; mvn herr
koma hinig af bragþi
oc brenna bæ firir Bvðlvngi.

20. Mvnatþv halda Hleiðrar
stoli, ra/þvm hringvm, ne reg-
ingrioti; tokvm a mondli,
mær! skarpara, ervma varmar
i valdreyra

21. Mol mins favþvr mær
ramliga, þviat hon feigð fira
fiolmargra sa; stvkkv storar
steðr fra lvdri, iarni varþar,
molvm enn framarr!

22. Let us grind more!
The son of the She-Bear on the
Half-Lords
will avenge Wisdom so that he
is famed both as her son
and as her brother
as we two know well."

22. Molvm enn framarr, mon
Yrsv sonr,
niðr Halfdanar, hefna Froþa;
sa mvn hennar heitinn verþa
bvrr oc broþir,
vitvm baþar þat.»

23. The Maidens ground,
empowered by rage, the young
girls
had the giant´s strength the
shaped wood shook the frame
collapsed
the heavy grindstone broke in
two.

23. Molv Meyiar, megins kost-
vþv, vorv vngar
i iotvnmoði; skvlfv skaptre,
ska/tz lvðr ofan, hravt hinn
havfgi hallr svndr i tvav.

24. And the Bride of the
Mountain Giant these words
spoke:
we have ground, Wisdom,
to the point where we must
stop for the ladies have had a
full stint of milling."

24. En Bergrisa
Brvðr orð vm qvað:
«Malit hofvm, Froþi! " sem
mvnvm hætta, hafa fvllstaþit
flioð at meldri.»

....

And before the song was over, they had ground an army against Wisdom, so that the same night there came that sea king who was called Mysingr [possibly "Of The Milk Serum"], and he killed Wisdom and took great booty there. And so the Peace of Wisdom was destroyed.

Mysing took with him the mill-stone Grotti and also The Heath Dweller and the Necklace Wearer and bid them grind salt, and by midnight the women asked if he had not had enough salt, but he asked them grind more. They kept grinding, and then the ship sank. In the ocean there was ever since a great abyss where the sea fell into the Mill´s eye. And this was when the ocean went salty.

...

oc aðr letti qvæþinv, molv þær her at Froþa, sva at á þeirri nott kom þar sa sækonungr, er Mysingr het, oc drap Froþa, toc þar herfang mikit. Þa lagþiz Froþafriþr.

Mysingr hafþi með ser Grotta oc sva Feniv oc Meniv oc bað þær mala salt, oc at miðri nott spvrþv þær, ef eigi leiddiz Mysingi salt; hann bað þær mala lengr. Þær molv litla hriþ, aðr niðr svkkv skipin, oc var þar eptir svelgr i hafinv, er særinn fellr i qvernara/gat; þa varð sær salltr.

Bronze Age Scandinavian rock carving showing the "Axe-god" raising his axe/hammer over an embracing couple. The Axe-god is most likely Thor's predecessor, and indeed, even in the Viking Age Thor was the god of marriages, consecrating the match with his hammer.

ALVÍSSMÁL - THE SPEECH OF THE ALL-KNOWING

ABOUT THE SPEECH OF THE ALL-KNOWING

This Edda poem reveals the multiple layers of cosmic dimensions where one thing may mean different things in each level of existence (or dimension). It is set in a typical Old Norse "word-duel"- a contest of wisdom, knowledge, wit and eloquence – the two duelers being the dwarf Allvíss [All-Knowing] and the god Thor [Þórr - "Thunder" – also a metaphor for the thinking mind].

The dwarf is seeking marriage with "the Bride", Thor's daughter. Apparently, the Bride's father is testing out the suitor to see if he is worthy of his daughter. From other sources we know that Thor's daughter was called Þrúðr, which means "Power". As all names are significant in Norse myths and all beings disguises for some deeper meanings, I think that the "dwarf" (a limited being) seeks to own or unite with a sort of "Power" associated with Thunder - by way of knowledge. And yet for all his knowledge he is outwitted by Thunder, who keeps the dwarf occupied until sunrise – the light of the Sun goddess turns the dwarf into stone.

This may in itself be a spiritual metaphor – the limited dwarf is no longer a limited dwarf but expanded and illuminated by the Sun´s light. In this translation I have aimed at translating as directly and literally as possible, including all names and place names. Thus it may sometimes sound a bit strange in English. However, you can find translations more adapted to the English language anywhere, and I am convinced that a literal translation will better enable us to truly understand Old Norse poetry and Old Norse perceptions.

ALVÍSSMÁL - THE SPEECH OF THE ALL-KNOWING

All-Knowing said;
1. ”Spread out the benches
now the Bride shall with me
turn on the road home
She was found in a hurry
many may think
- it is at home that one may
find peace”

Alvíss qvaþ:
1. «Becki breiþa,
nv scal Brvþr meþ mer
heim i sinni snvaz;
hrataþ vm mégi
mvn hveriom þiccia,
heima scalat hvíld nema.»

Thor said;
2. ”Who is this vagabond
”Why are you so pale around
the nose?
Were you this night with a
corpse?
The like of a troll
you seem to be to me:
You were not born for a Bride”

Þórr qvaþ:
2. «Hvat er þat fira?
hví ertv sva fa/lr vm nasar?
vartv i nótt meþ ná?
þvrsa líci
þicci mer a þer vera;
ertattv til Brvþar borinn.»

All-Knowing said;
3. ”My name is All-Knowing
I live beneath the Earth
by
and my place is beneath the
rocks
to the fields of men
did I come from far and wide
may no man break a given
word

Alvíss qvaþ:
3. «Alvíss ec heiti,
ec fyr iorþ neþan,
a ec vndir steini staþ;
vagna vers
ec em a vit kominn;
bregði engi fa/sto heiti fira!»

Thor said:
4. "I may break (the word)
for I own the Bride
and as her father I have that
power
I was not home
when she was promised to you
when that match was made
among the gods

All Knowing said:
5. "Who is that warrior
who wants to rule
over the beautiful and fair
glowing (Bride)?
a homeless hobo
few people must know about
you
who has given you
the arm-rings you wear?"

Thor said:
6. "Victorious/Battle Thor is
my name
I have traveled widely
I am the son of Broad Beard
and with my consent shall you
never
have that young maiden
or get that marriage-word."

All-Knowing said:
7. "Your consent
is one that I will have swiftly
and get that marriage-word
I will rather hold
than be without
that Flour White Maiden."

Thor said:
8. "The Maiden´s promise
may be yours
wise guest! If it is so
that you can from all
the worlds tell (me)
all that I wish to know:

Þórr qvaþ:
4.«Ec mvn bregda,
þviat ec Brvþar a
flest vm ráþ sem faþir; varca
ec heima,
þa er þer heitiþ var,
at sa einn er
gia/fer meþ godom.»

Alvíss qvaþ:
5. «Hvat er þat recca,
er i raþom telz
flioþs ens fagrgloa?
fiarrafleina
þic mvno fair kvnna;
hverr hefir þic
ba/gom borit?»

Þórr qvaþ: 6.«Vingþórr ec
heiti,
ec hefi viþa rataþ,
sonr em ec Siþgrana;
at osatt minni scalattv
þat iþ vnga man hafa
oc þat giaforþ geta.»

Alvíss qvaþ:
7. «Sattir þinar
er ec vil snemma hafa
oc þat giaforþ geta;
eiga vilia heldr
enn án vera
þat iþ Miallhvita Man.»

Þórr qvaþ:
8. «Meyiar astom
mvna þer verþa,
visi gestr! of variþ,
ef þv or heimi kant
hveriom at segia
alt þat er ec vil vita:

9. Tell me this, All-Knowing
how everything is made.
I want, dwarf, to know it!
What is the Earth called
-who lies before the sons of
the ages-
in all the worlds?"

All-Knowing said:
10. "Earth she is called
among men
and with the Aesir, Land
she is Paths among the Vanir
Ever-Green to the giants
Growing to the elves
the High Powers call her Mud-
Sand"110

Thor said:
11. "Tell me this, All-Knowing
how everything is made.
I want, dwarf, to know it!
What Heaven is called
-so widely known-
in all the worlds?"

All-Wise said:
12. "Heaven he is called
among men
and Sibling Lights (stars, planets) with the gods
Wind-Weaver among the
Vanir
World Above to the giants
To elves the Beautiful Roof
to dwarfs the Dripping Hall."

Thor said:
13. «Tell met his, All-Knowing
how everything is made.
I want, dwarf, to know it!
What the Moon is called
-the one that people can see -
in all the worlds?"

9. Segðv mer þat, Alvíss!
oll of ra/c fira
voromc, dvergr! at vitir:
hve sv Iorþ heitir,
er liggr fyr alda sonom,
heimi hveriom i?»

Alvíss qvaþ:
10. «Iorþ heitir
meþ monnom,
en meþ asom Fold,
calla Vega vanir,
igron iotnar,
alfar Groandi,
kalla Aur vpregin.»

Þórr qvaþ:
11. «Segdv mer þat, Alvíss!
oll of ra/c fira,
voromc, dvergr! at vitir:
hve sa Himinn heitir,
erakendi,
heimi hveriom i?»

Alvíss qvaþ:
«Himinn heitir
meþ monnom,
en Hlyrnir meþ godom,
kalla Vindofni vanir,
Uppheim iotnar,
alfar Fagra Refr,
dvergar Drivpan Sal.»

Þórr qvaþ:
13. «Segðv mer þat, Alvíss!
oll of ra/c fira
voromc, dvergr! at vitir:
hverso máni heitir,
sa er menn sia,
heimi hveriom i?»

All-Knowing said:
14. "Moon he is called
among men
and Waning among the gods
he is called the Whirling
Wheel in Death
Hastener among giants
Shine among the dwarfs
the elves call him Year Count-
er."

Thor said:
15. "Tell me this, All-Knowing
how everything is made.
I want, dwarf, to know it!
What the Sun is called
-the one visible to the sons of
the ages -
in all the worlds?"

All Knowing said:
16. "Sol she is called
among men
and Sunna among the gods
the dwarfs call her the Hiber-
nation´s Lover
Eternal Glow she is to the
giants
Beautiful Wheel to the elves
All-Transparent to the sons of
the Aesir."

Thor said:
17. "Tell me this, All-Knowing
how everything is made.
I want, dwarf, to know it!
What are the clouds called
-blended with rain showers -
in all the worlds?"

Alvíss qvaþ:
14. «Mani heitir
meþ monnom,
en Mylinn meþ godom,
kalla Hverfanda Hvel Helio i,
Scyndi iotnar,
en Scin dvergar,
kalla alfar Artala.»

Þórr qvaþ:
15. «Segðv mer þat, Alvíss!
oll of ra/c fira
voromc, dvergr! at vitir:
hve sv Sol heitir,
er sia alda synir,
heimi hveriom i?»

Alvíss qvaþ:
16. «Sol heitir
meþ monnom,
enn svnna meþ goþom,
kalla dvergar Dvalins leica,
Eyglo iotnar,
alfar Fagra Hvel,
Alscír asa synir.»

Þórr qvaþ:
17. «Segðv mer þat, Alvíss!
oll of ra/c fira
voromc, dvergr! at vitir:
hve þa/ scy heita,
er scvrom blandaz,
heimi hveriom i?

All Knowing said:
18. "Clouds they are called
among men
and Rain-Hope with the gods
called Wind-Floaters among
the Vanir
Original Hope with the giants
with elves they are the Wind
Power
called in Death the Concealing
Helmet."

Thor said:

19. "Tell me this, All-Knowing
how everything is made.
I want, dwarf, to know it!
What is the Wind called
-that travels most widely -
in all the worlds?"

All Knowing said:
20. "Wind he is called
among men
and Waving with the gods
called Neighing among the
Sacred Rulers
Howling to the giants
To the elves, Sound-Traveler
called in Death the
Storm-Maker."

Thor said:
21. "Tell me this, All-Knowing
how everything is made.
I want, dwarf, to know it!
What is that Calm called
that shall descend
in all the worlds?"

Alvíss qvaþ:
18. «Scy heitir
með monnom,
enn Scvrvan með goðom,
kalla Vindflot vanir,
Urván iotnar,
alfar Veþrmegin,
kalla i Helio Hialm Hvliz.»

Þórr qvaþ:

19. «Segðv mer þat, Alvíss!
oll of ra/c fira
voromc, dvergr! at vitir:
hve sa vindr heitir,
er viðast ferr,
heimi hveriom i?»

Alvíss qvaþ:
20. «Vindr heitir
með monnom,
enn Vávoþr með goðom,
kalla Gneggioþ ginnregin,
opi ia/tnar,
alfar dynfara,
kalla i Helio Hviþvþ.»

Þórr qvaþ:
21. «Segðv mer þat, Alvíss!
oll of ra/c fira
voromc, dvergr! at vitir:
hve þat Logn heitir,
er liggia scal,
heimi hveriom i?»

All Knowing said:
22. "Calm it is called
among men
and Light with the gods
called Wind-End with the Vanir
Too Hot for the giants
To elves the End of Day
to dwarfs the Peace of Day."

Thor said:
23. "Tell me this, All-Knowing
how everything is made.
I want, dwarf, to know it!
What is the Ocean called
that men are rowing
in all the worlds?"

All Knowing said:
24. Sea he is called
among men
Illusion[111] with the gods
called Wave among the Vanir
Ale World to the giants
to the elves, Staff of Laws
to the dwarfs the Dripping Steed."

Thor said:
25. "Tell me this, All-Knowing
how everything is made.
I want, dwarf, to know it!
What is the Fire called
that burns for the children of the ages
in all the worlds?

All Knowing said:
26."Fire he is called
among men
and with the Aesir, Spark
called Burner among Vanir
Greedy to the giants
and Burning Up to the dwarfs
called in Death the Hastener."

Alvíss qvaþ:
22. «Logn heitir
meþ monnom,
enn Logi meþ goðom,
kalla Vindslot vanir,
Ofhlý iotnar,
alfar Dagseva,
kalla dvergar dags vero.»

Þórr qvaþ:
23. «Segðv mer þat, Alvíss!
oll of ra/c fira
voromc, dvergr! at vitir:
hve sa marr heitir,
er menn roa,
heimi hveriom i?»

Alvíss qvaþ:
24. «Ser heitir
meþ monnom,
en Silegia meþ goþom,
kalla Vág vanir,
Álheim iotnar,
alfar Lagastaf,
kalla dvergar Divpan Mar.»

Þórr qvaþ:
25. «Segðv mer þat, Alvíss!
oll of ra/c fira
voromc, dvergr! at vitir:
hve sa eldr heitir,
er brenn fyr alda sonom,
heimi hveriom i?»

Alvíss qvaþ:
26. «Eldr heitir
meþ monnom,
enn meþ asom Fvni,
kalla Vag vanir,
Frekan iotnar,
en Forbrenni dvergar,
kalla i Helio Hra/þvþ.»

Thor said:
27. "Tell me this, All-Knowing
how everything is made.
I want, dwarf, to know it!
What is that Forest called
that grows for the children of
the age
in all the worlds?"

All Knowing said:
28. "Wood it is called
among men
and Mane of Hills among gods
called Rock-Seaweed among
people
Timber among giants
to the elves, Beautiful Twig
called Wand by the Vanir."

Thor said:
29. "Tell me this, All-Knowing
how everything is made.
I want, dwarf, to know it!
What the Night is called
she who is known to the
Northerner
in all the worlds?"

All Knowing said
30. "Night she is called
among men
and Darkness among gods
called Disguiser among the
Sacred Powers
Un-Light by the giants
to the elves, Sleep Pleasure
to the dwarfs, Dream God-
dess."

Thor said:
31. "Tell me this, All-Knowing
how everything is made.
I want, dwarf, to know it!
What is that Seed called
that is sown by the sons of the
ages
in all the worlds?"

Þórr qvaþ:
27. «Segðv mer þat, Alvíss!
oll of ra/c fira
voromc, dvergr! at vitir:
hve sa viþr heitir,
er vex fyr alda sonom,
heimi hveriom i?»

Alvíss qvaþ:
28. «Viþr heitir
meþ monnom,
enn Vallar Fax meþ goðom,
kalla Hliþþang halir,
Elldi iotnar,
alfar Fagrlima,
kalla vond vanir.»

Þórr qvaþ:
29. «Segðv mer þat, Alvíss!
oll of ra/c fira
voromc, dvergr! at vitir:
hve sva Nótt heitir,
en Na/rvi kenda,
heimi hveriom i?»

Alvíss qvaþ:
30. «Nott heitir
meþ monnom,
en Niól meþ goðom,
kalla Grimo ginnregin,
Oliós iotnar,
alfar svefngaman,
kalla dvergar Draumniorvn.»

Þórr qvaþ:
31. «Segðv mer þat, Alvíss!
oll of ra/c fira
voromc, dvergr! at vitir:
hve þat Sáþ heitir,
er sá alda synir,
heimi hveriom i?»

All Knowing said:
32. «Barley it is called
among men
and Conifer among the gods
Called Growth by the Vanir
Food to the giants
Staff of Laws to the elves
called in Death the Hanging
Head.”

Thor said:
33. ”Tell me this, All-Knowing
how everything is made.
I want, dwarf, to know it!
What is that Ale called
that is drunk by the children
of the ages
in all the worlds?”

All Knowing said:
34. ”Ale it is called
among men
and with the Aesir Beer
called Power Drink by the
Vanir
Clear Brew to the giants
and in Death, Mead
called Brew by the sons of
Heavy With Drink.”

Thor said:
35. «In one single chest
I never saw
more ancient runes
With much talk
I spoke beguilement for you
You are up, dwarf, it is dawn
now Sun shines in the hall.”

Alvíss qvaþ:
32. «Bygg heitir
meþ monnom,
enn Barr meþ goðom,
kalla Vaxt vanir,
eti ia/tnar,
alfar lagastaf,
kalla i Helio Hnipinn.»

Þórr qvaþ:
33. «Segðv mer þat, Alvíss!
oll of ra/c fira
voromc, dvergr! at vitir:
hve þat Aul heitir,
er drecca alda synir,
heimi hveriom i?»

Alvíss qvaþ:
34. «Ol heitir
meþ monnom,
enn meþ asom Biórr,
kalla Veig vanir,
hreina la/g ia/tnar,
enn i Helio Mioþ,
kalla svmbl Svttvngs synir.»

Þórr qvaþ:
35. «I eino briosti
ec sác aldregi
fleiri forna stafi;
miclom talom
ec qveð teldan þic:
vppi ertv, dvergr! vm dagaþr,
nv scinn Sól i sali.»

HYNDLULIÓÐ

THE SONG OF THE SHE-WOLF

In this poem, a young man called Óttarr (Fear-Warrior) makes sacrifice to the goddess Freyia, who appears before him as the stones of the altar he has built turn into crystal. She transforms him into the sacrificial boar, recently dead, and rides him into the Underworld where she meets her deadly alter-ego, Hyndla (The She- Wolf), who is a representative of Hel and death. There, she convinces the wolf- riding ogress to reveal all the secrets of the world´s lineages and their unity and common origin, so that he may, on "the third morning" (after the initiation) may contend with his opponent Angantýr (Beast/God of Pleasure). This is one of the initiation poems in the Poetic Edda, including the serving of the precious mead of memory. Hyndla, as a wolf-riding goddess, is identifiable with another ogress, Hýrokkin (Fire-Spinner), an ogress of death riding wolves and having serpents for reins, and she is stronger than all the gods together.

The Lady chanted:
1. Wake, oh Maiden among Maidens
Wake up, my friend,She-Wolf, Sister!
- who lives in the rock-cave;
Now is the darkness of darkness itself[112]
We together ought to ride to the Hall of the Chosen [Valhalla]
and to the sacred shrine

2. We shall bid the Father of Hosts[113] that we two be seated in his mind/intent:- He owes and gives
 the gold of the world´s children
He gave to Hermóðr[114]
helmet and armor and to Sigmund[r115] a sword to keep.

1. Freyia qvaþ:
"Vaki mær meyia, vaki min vina, Hyndla systir!
er i helli byr;
nu er rauckr rauckra, rida vit skulum
til Valhallar
ok til vess heilags.

2. Bidium Heriafaudur i hugum sitia;
hann gelldr ok gefr gull ver- dungu;
gaf hann Hermodi hialm ok bryniu, enn Sigmundi suerd at þiggia.

3. He gives victory to some and
to others, abundance eloquence
to many and common sense to
all people
Wind he gives to follow sailors
and inspiration to the poets
He gives a man´s courage to
many a warrior.

4. To Þórr she must sacrifice
and this must she ask for that
he by you will act kindly though
he is often known to be hos-
tile towards the brides of the
Devourer

5. Now take you your wolf
one from your stable
and let him run
alongside my steed."
The She-Wolf chanted:
"Late will your boar
walk the path of the gods
I will not allow my steed to be
exhausted.

6. False are you, Freyia and you
are testing me you show in your
eyes
when you look at us that way
that you are taking your man
on the path of the Chosen Dead,
Fear-Warrior the young,
Within-Matter´s son."[116]

7. Freyia said:
"Confused are you, She-Wolf!
Dreams must be having you,
when you think I am taking
my man on the path of the Chosen Dead;
This is my glowing boar
the golden-bridled Battle-Swine
He was made for me by the two
dwarfs known as Dying and
Close-Call.

3. Gefr hann sigr sonum,
en summum aura, mælsku
morgum
ok mannvit firum;
byri gefr hann braugnum, enn
brag skældum,
gefr hann mannsemi morgum
recki.

4. Þor mun hon blota, þess mun
hon bidia, at hann æ vid þik
einart laati;
þo er honum otijtt vid iotuns
brudir.

5. Nu taktu vlf þinn einn af
stalli,
læt hann renna med runa
minum."
Hyndla qvaþ:
"Seinn er gaulltr þinn godveg
troda,
vilkat ek mar minn mætann
hleda.

6. Fla ertu, Freyia! er þu freis-
tar min, visar þu augum
a oss þannig,
er þu hefir ver þinn i valsinne,
Ottar unga, Innsteins bur.»

Freyia kvað:
7. «Dulin ertu, Hyndla! draums
ætlig þer,
er þu kuedr ver minn i valsinni,
þar er gaulltr gloar gullinbusti
Hilldisuine, er mer hagir giordu
duergar tueir,
Dainn ok Nabbi.

8. We should dismount to talk about this and sit down together about lineages we should pass verdict about the high-born and those descended from the gods.

9. They have wagered for the gold of the Chosen117; Fear-Warrior the young and the God of Pleasure; He is owed to know so that the young champion may have his father´s legacy after his kinsfolk.

10. An altar did he make for me made out of stones [matter/grave]
-now the rocks have been turned into crystal – Crimson he colored it with the blood of the sacrifice Fear-Warrior always put his faith in [us] goddesses.

11. Now let us count up the ancestors and the lineages of men born from them What are the Shield-Descendants? What are the Shiver-Descendants? What are the Abundance-Descendants? What are the Wolf [Desire]-Descendants? What are the Flesh-Born? What are the Ruler-Born? What is the best Choice of men in Middle Earth?»

8. Sennum vit or sodlum, sitia vit skulum ok vm iofra ættir dæma, gumna þeirra er fra godum kuomu.

9. Þeir hafa vediat Vala malmi Ottar ungi ok Angantyr; skyllt er at veita, sua at skati enn vngi faudurleifd hafui eftir frændr sina

10. Haurg hann mer gerdi hladinn steinum — nu er griot þat at gleri vordit —, raud hann i nyiu nauta blodi, æ trvdi Ottar a asyniur.

11. Nu lattu forna nidia talda ok vpp bornar ættir manna: huat er Skiolldunga, huat er Skilfinga, huat er Audlinga, huat er Ylfinga, huat er haulldborit, huat er hersborit, mest manna val vnd Midgardi?»

12. The She-Wolf said:

«You are Fear-Warrior born to
Within-Matter
Within-Matter was born from
Soul the Old Soul from Wolf,
Wolf from the Sea-Traveler
And Sea-Traveler was born from
Swan the Red[118]

13. Your father had a mother
adorned with necklaces
I think her name was
Wind-Shielded-Goddess, the
priestess;[119] Their father was
Wisdom
and Love their mother; All that
lineage belongs to the people
above.

14. Choice[120] was before the
most prominent of men
Before him, the High-Elf-Lord
was the highest of the
Shield-Descendants;
Famous were the people-wars
that these men led
his deeds were widely famous
up to the vault of heaven.

15. He made, with Is-
land-Source,
- the best among men-
and he killed Victory-Certainty
with cool edges Then he went to
own Elm-Power-Drink
-the best among women –
they made together and owned
eighteen sons.

12. Hyndla kvað:

«Þu ert, Ottar! borinn Innstei-
ni, enn Innsteinn var Aalfui
enum gamla; Aalfr var Vlfui,
Vlfr Sæfara, enn Sæfari
Suan enum rauda

13. Modur atti fadir þinn meni-
um gaufga,
hygg ek at hon heti Hledis
gydia;
Frodi var fadir þeirrar, enn †
Friaut modir; aull þotti ætt su
med yfirmonnum.

14. Vali var adr auflgazstr
manna, Halfdan fyrri hæstr
Skiolldunga; fræg voru folkvig
þau er framir gerdu, huarfla
þottu hans verk med himins
skautum.

15. Efldiz hann vid Eymund
æzstann manna,
enn hann vo Sigtrygg med
suolum eggium; eiga geck Aal-
mueig æzsta quinna,
olu þau ok attu atian sonu.

16. From them are the
Shield-Descendants From them
are the Shiver-Descendants
From them are the Abun-
dance-Descendants From them
are the Flesh-Born
From them are the Ruler-Born
-best Choice of men in Middle
Earth
and they are all your kind,
Fear-Warrior of the narrow
mind!

17. Battle-Combat was her
mother,[121] daughter of Sleeping
Woman
and the Sea-King[122];
and they are all your kind,
Fear-Warrior of the narrow
mind!
-Knowing this is worthwhile, do
you want to know further?

18. Day married Thunder-Wom-
an
-mother of champions – that
lineage created
the greatest of fighters; Furi-
ous-Ocean and Girdle and both
the Greeds,
Dark and Yeast-Ocean, Soul the
Old;[123]
-Knowing this is worthwhile, do
you want to know further?

19. Kettle[124] was their friend,
heir to Skillfulness,
he was the father of the mother
of your mother;
There was Wisdom
before him Gust-of-Wind[125] the
elder son he was
born to Soul.

16. Þadan eru Skiolldungar,
þadan eru Skilfingar,
þadan Audlingar, þadan
Ynglingar, þadan haulldborit,
þadan hersborit, mest manna
val vnd Midgardi;
allt er þat ætt þin, Ottar heims-
ki!

17. Var Hilldigunn hennar modir Suofu barn
ok Sækonungs; allt er þat ætt
þin, Ottar heimski!
vardar at viti sua, viltu enn
leingra?

18. Dagr atti Þoru drengia
modur, oluzst i ætt þar æzstir
kappar: Fradmarr ok Gyrdr ok
Frekar badir, Ámr ok Iosur-
mar, Aalfr enn gamli;
vardar at viti sua, villtu enn
leingra?

19. Ketill het vinr þeirra Klyps
arfþegi,
var hann modurfadir modur
þinnar;
þar var Frodi fyrr enn Kari,
hinn elldri var Aalfr vm getinn

20. Nanna[126] came next, then, the daughter of Dark-ness-Shrine,
her kinsman was the kinsman of your father Forgotten is that kindship,
I can speak further; I knew them both,
Arrowhead and Linen-Bow-string[127]
-and they are all your kind, Fear-Warrior of the narrow mind!

21. Ice-Wolf and Divine Wolf sons of Ale-Courage
with Arrow-Shower-Battle, daughter of the Slanting/Lop-sided One,
a large number of kinsmen you must count;
-and they are all your kind, Fear-Warrior of the narrow mind!

22.Battle-Warrior the bulwark Masked-One the Legacy-getter Daring-One the Ironshielded Greed the Gaping.

23. Army-Guardian, Herd-Guardian Robberer and Beast-of-Pleasure Resident and Eyelash,
Conifer and Joy-Enhancer Peak and Peat-Covered and the two Hairy-Heads;
-and they are all your kind, Fear-Warrior of the narrow mind!

20. Nanna var næst þar Nauck-ua dottir,
var maugr hennar magr þins faudur; fyrnd er su mægd,
fram tel ek leingra: kunna ek bada Brodd ok Haurfi;
allt er þat ætt þin, Ottar heims-ki!

21.Isolfr ok Aasolfr Aulmods synir
ok Skurhilldar Skeckils dottur, skaltu til telia skatna margra;
allt er þat ætt þin, Ottar heims-ki!

22. Gunnar balkr, Grimr ar-dskafui, iarnskiolldr Þorir, Vlfr ginandi.

23. [Hervardr, Hiorvardr, Hra-ni, Angantyr,]
Bui ok Brami, Barri ok Reifnir, Tindr ok Tyrfingr
ok tueir Haddingiar;
allt er þat ætt þin, Ottar heims-ki!

24. East in Bear-Island they
were born,
the sons of Eagle-Masked[128]
with Island-Furrow;
The noise of berserkers with
tidings of un-peace across lands
and seas the fire was loose
-and they are all your kind,
Fear-Warrior of the narrow
mind!

25. I knew both Arrowhead and
Linen-Bowstring they were in
the army of Famous-Wolf the
old[129] all these were born
from the Great-Traveler
the kinsman of Sígurðr [Victory
Origin][130]
-pay attention to my wisdom! -
to the Masked One´s folk
who slayed the Embracer.[131]

26. He [Sígurðr] was descended
from the Sacred-Wand-Descen-
dant[132] and Herd-Goddess [his
mother]
from the Destructive-Descen-
dants
and Joiner-of-Islands [making
worlds come together] from the
Abundance-Descendants;
-and they are all your kind,
Fear-Warrior of the narrow
mind!

24. Austr i Bolm voru bornir,
Arngrims synir ok Eyfuru;
braukun berserkia bauls marg-
skonar vm laund ok vm laug
sem logi færi;
allt er þat ætt þin, Ottar heims-
ki!

25. Kunna ek bæda Brodd ok
Haurfi, voru þeir i hird Hrolfs
ens gamla.
Allir bornir fra Iormunreki
Sigurdar mægi,
— hlyd þu saugu minni! —
folkum grims þess er Fafni uǫ.

26.Sa var visir fra Vaulsungi ok
Hiordis
fra Hraudungi, enn Eylimi
fra Audlingum;
allt er þat ætt þin, Ottar heims-
ki!

27. Battle-Warrior and Thinker, heirs to Giuki,
and the same was Divine Symbol/Fate, their sister,
Divine Mercy was not of the kindred of Giuki
although he was the brother of them both[133]
-and they are all your kind, Fear-Warrior of the narrow mind!

28. Harald Wartooth was born to Hrærek that generous hurler of rings,
He [Harald] was the son of Aud [Abundance], Aud the Deep-Minded, Ivarr´s daughter,
And Rádbard [Council-Beard] was the father of Randver [Shield-Man];[134]
They were men blessed much by the gods
-and they are all your kind, Fear-Warrior of the narrow mind!

29. Eleven was the number of Aesir counted,
when Baldr had slumped against his hammock of Death [there used to be twelve]; To this [loss/incompletion]
was The Choice born to avenge his brother, he slew the killer[135]
-and they are all your kind, Fear-Warrior of the narrow mind!

27. Gunnarr ok Haugni Giuka arfar,
ok id sama Gudrun systir þeirra:
eigi var Guthormr Giuka ættar,
þo var hann brodir beggia þeirra;
allt er þat ætt þin, Ottar heimski!

28. Haralldr hillditaunn borinn Hræreki slaunguanbauga,
sonr var hann Audar,
Audr diupudga , Ifuars dottir,
enn Radbardr var Randués fadir; þeir voru gumnar godum signadir;
allt er þat ætt þin, Ottar heimski!

29. Voru ellifu æsir taldir, Balldr er hne vid banaþufu; þess letz Vali verdr at hefna, sins brodur
slo hann handbana;
allt er þat ætt þin, Ottar heimski!

30. Baldr´s father [Óðinn] was the heir of Storage Chamber Freyr [growth] married Enclosure,
she was the daughter of Hides-Something, of the lineage of the Devourers,
and [she was the daughter] of Bids-Rock-Matter[136]; though the Slave-Binder was their kinsman, that Devourer so fond of shooting; his daughter was Injury.[137]

31. Much have we [Freyia and Hyndla] told you and more shall we tell
-Knowing this is worthwhile, do you want to know further?

32. Hook was the best by far of the sons of the She-Goat[138] and the She-Goat´s father was Herd-Guardian;
Bright-Open-Space and Horse-Thief139 kindred of the Burned One

33. All wand-witches are descended from Wood-Desire[140] all wizards
from the Tree of Will all magic-wombs from Dark Mind all Devourers from Sound.[141]

34. Much have we told you and more shall we tell
-Knowing this is worthwhile, do you want to know further?

35. One was born
in the days before time immensely powerful of the rulers´ kind:
Nine [mothers] gave birth to the magnificent man [Nine] giant maidens
by the edge of the world[142]

30. Var Balldrs fadir Burs arfþegi,
Freyr atti Gerdi,
hon var Gymis dottir, iotna ættar,
ok Aurbodu; þo var Þiassi þeirra frændi
skautgiarn iotun, hans var Skadi dottir.

31. Mart segium þer ok munum fleira, vorumz at viti sua, villtu enn leingra?

32. Haki var Huædnu hoti bezstr sona,
enn Huednu var Hiorvardr fadir; Heidr ok Hrossþiofr Hrimnis kindar.

33. Eru vaulur allar fra Vidolfui,
vitkar allir fra Vilmeidi, seid-berendr
fra Suarthofda, iotnar allir fra Ymi komnir.

34.Mart segium þer ok munum fleira, vorumzst at viti sua, villtu enn leingra?

35. Vard einn borin i ardaga rammaukin miok raugna kindar;
niu baru þann naddgaufgann mann iotna meyiar
vid iardar þraum.

36. Much have we told you and more shall we tell
-Knowing this is worthwhile, do you want to know further?

37. Howling One birthed him, Grasping One birthed him, the Achiever birthed him, and the Giver of Wealth,
Wolf-Rune [Desire-Fate] birthed him and Pleasure-Island,
She-Wolf and Intender and Iron-Scissors.

38. He was strengthened to grow by the power of Earth
by the cool-cold Sea
and the blood of the Atonement.

39. Much have we told you and more shall we tell
-Knowing this is worthwhile, do you want to know further?

40. Wolf bore Loki
by She-Who-Bids-Anger and he had Glider [Sleipnir] by Misfortune-Travler;
One child [of Loki´s]
is thought to be the worst,
he was descended from the brother of Lightning Storm[143]

41. Loki ate from the heart burnt on the linden [woman] fire[144] He found there half-torched
the soulstone of the woman;
The Lofty One [Loki] was impregnated by that wicked woman;
from this act, to the Earth has come all bad things.

36. Mart segium þer ok munum fleira, vorumz at viti sua, villtu enn leingra?

37. Hann Gialp vm bar, hann Greip vm bar,
bar hann Eistla ok Eyrgiafa,
hann bar Vlfrun ok Angeyia,
Imdr ok Atla ok Iarnsaxa

38. Sa var aukinn iardar megni, sualkaulldum sæ ok sonard-reyra.

39. Mart segium þer ok munum fleira, vǫrumz at viti sua, villtu enn leingra?

40. Ol vlf Loki vid Angrbodu, enn Sleipni gat vid Suadilfara; eitt þotti skars allra feiknazst, þat var brodur fra Byleistz komit.

41. Loki af hiarta lindi brendu, fann hann halfsuidinn hug-stein konu;
vard Loptr kuidugr af konu illri; þadan er a folldu flagd huert komit.

42. The ocean stirs up storms
against Heaven itself
washes over the lands and the
air itself yields;
from there come the snows and
the biting winds
it is decreed thus [by the norns]
that the rulers will fall.

43. One was born greater than
all
he was made to grow by the
power of Earth It is said that he
is the one of greatest power
and that every being, all related,
come together from him.[145]

44. Then comes another even
mightier,
though I do not dare to men-
tion his name; Few can now see
further than this
than when Spirit must fight the
Wolf of Greed.”

Freyia said:
45. ”Carry the Ale of Memory to
my guest
so that he can hold on to all
your words
of this council
on the third morning
when he must contend in lineages with the Beast of Pleasure.”

The She-Wolf said:
46. ”Turn swiftly back where
you came from! Sleep is all I
want
Few fair things of value
shall you [Fear-Warrior] have
from me. You run, noble girlfriend [Freyia], outside at nights
just like when Bright-Open-
Space-Symbol runs with the
bucks.[146]

42. Haf gengr hridum vid
himin sialfann, lidr lond yfir,
enn loft bilar; þadan koma
sniofar ok snarir vindar,
þa er i radi,
at regn vm þrioti.

43. Vard einn borinn aullum
meiri,
sa var aukinn iardar megni;
þann kueda stilli storaudgaz-
stann, sif sifiadann siotum
giorfaullum

44. Þa kemr annar enn mat-
kari,
þo þori ek eigi þann at nefna;
fair sia nu
fram vm leingra, enn Óðinnn
man vlfui mæta.»

Freyia kvað:
45. «Ber þu minnis aul minum
gesti,
sua hann aull mune ord at tina
þersar rædu
a þridia morni,
þa er þeir Angantyr ættir
rekia.»

Hyndla kvað:
46. «Snudu braut hedan! sofua
lystir mik,
fær þu fatt af mer fridra kosta;
hleypr þu, edlvina! vti a nattum,
sem med haufrum Heidrun
fari.

47.nYou ran after Poetry/Spirit always desiring [it]
Still many more are known
to have sought up beneath your skirts;
You run, noble girlfriend outside at nights
just like when Bright-Open-Space-Symbol runs with the bucks.

Freyia said:
48. "I throw a fire
around the Witches-Within-in-Wood, so that you can
never come out unburnt, from here."[147]

She-Wolf said:
49. "I see a fire burn and the Earth aflame
most will try to ransom their lives when suffering;
You [Freyia] carry, to Fear-Warrior, the precious drink
-(but) it is blended with poison and ill fortune."

Freyia said:
50. "Your cursing words
shall not be ruling [this outcome] even if you, bride of Devourers intend to call down the worst The precious power-drink
I shall bid Fear-Warrior to drink and I bid all the gods to help him."[148]

47. Rant at Odi ey þreyiandi,
skutuzst þer fleiri vnd fyrirskyrtu;
hleypr þu, edlvina! vti a nattum,
sem med haufrum Heidrun fari.»

Freyia kvað:
48. «Ek slæ elldi of ividiu,
sua at þu eigi kemz a braut hedan;

Hyndla kvað:
49. Hyr se ek brenna enn haudr loga, verda flestir fiorlausn þola;
ber þu Ottari bior at hendi eitri blandinn miok illu heilli.»

Freyia kvað:
50. «Ordheill þin skal engu rada,
þottu, brudr iotuns! baulfui heitir;
hann skal drecka dyrar veigar,
bid ek Ottari aull god duga.»

BIBLIOGRAPHY

Acker, Paul/ Larrington,Carolyne (red.) (2002): The Poetic Edda: essays on Old Norse mythology - Routledge Medieval Casebooks, New York

Ahlbäck, Tore (ed.) (1990):Old Norse and Finnish Religions and Cultic Place- Names -Almqvist & Wiksell International, Stockholm

Bugge, Sophus, red. (1867 / 1965): SÆMUNDAR EDDA HINS FRÓDA - Norrøn Fornkvædi -Islandsk Samling av Folkelige Oldtidsdigte om Nordens Guder og Heroer - Universitetsforlaget, Oslo

Bugge, Sophus (1867): Sæmundar Edda - Available online: http://etext.old.no/

Clunies-Ross, Margaret (1987). Skáldskaparmál –Snorri Sturlusson`s Ars Poetica and Medieval Theories of Language Odense University Press

Clunies-Ross, Margaret (1994): Prolongued Echoes -Old Norse Myths in Medieval Northern Society, Volume I: The Myths - Odense University Press

Den Arnamagnæanske Kommision (1989): Ordbog over det norrøne prosasprog/ A Dictionary of Old Norse Prose – Vol. I – XII – København

Dronke, Ursula (1997):The Poetic Edda, volume II: Mythological Poems Clarendon Press, Oxford

Eggen, Erik (1978):Snorre Sturluson: Den yngre Edda Det Norske Samlaget, Oslo

Eliade, Mircea (1965): Rites and Symbols of Initiation: the mysteries of birth and rebirth - Harper torchbooks Harper Colophon Books, New York: Harper & Row
Enright, Michael J. (1996): Lady with a Mead Cup -Ritual, Prophecy and Lordship in the European Warband from La Tène to the Viking Age Four Courts Press, Dublin

Faulkes, Anthony (1987): Snorri Sturluson: EDDA Snorri Sturluson - University of Birmingham Everyman, London

Fisher, Peter (Translation)/Ellis Davidson, Hilda(Ed.) (1996): Saxo Grammaticus: The history of the Danes - Books I-IX /

Flint, Valerie I. J. (1991): The Rise of Magic in Early Medieval Europe. Princeton

Flood, Jan Peder (1999): Volver, Seidmenn og Sjamaner: en komparativ analyse av norrøn seid- Hovedoppgave i religionshistorie, Universitetet i Oslo

Fritzner, Johan (1886): Ordbog over det gamle norske sprog – Det norske forlags forening

Fritzner, Johan (1972): Ordbog over det gamle norske sprog – rettelser og tillegg. Universitetsforlaget

Gyldendal Norsk Forlag (1944) Snorri Sturlusson: Snorres Kongesagaer (Heimskringla, Ynglinga Saga), Oslo

Heggestad/Hødnebø/Simensen (1975): Norrøn Ordbok – Det norske samlaget

Hollander, Lee M. (1986): The Poetic Edda University of Texas Press, Austin

Hólmarsson, Sverrir /Sanders, Christopher / Tucker, John (1989): Íslensk-ensk orðabók – ráðgjöf: Svavar Sigmundsson – Orðabækur Iðunnar, Reykjavik

Holm-Olsen, Ludvig (1985): Eddadikt Cappelen, Trondheim

Hoppál Mihaly/ Pentikäinen, Juha (eds.)(1992): NORTHERN RELIGIONS AND SHAMANISM - ETHNOLOGICA URALICA 3 Budapest Akadémiai Kiadó, Helsinki Finnish Literature Society
Iversen, Ragnvald (1972-1994): Norrøn grammatikk - Tano

Jannson, Sven (1986): Isländsk-Svensk Ordbog – Göteborg

Jónsson, Finnur, ed. (1907): EDDA Snorra Sturlusonar Reykjavik

Jónsson, Finnur, ed.(1912): Den Norsk-Islandske Skjaldedigtning (800-1200) udgiven af Kommisjonen for det Arnamagnæisk legat B: rettet tekst, 1. bind Gyldendalske Boghandel –Nordisk Forlag København og Kristiania

Larrington, Carolyne (1996): The Poetic Edda Oxford University Press, Oxford, New York

Lind, E.H (1920-1921): Norsk-Isländska Person-Binamn, Uppsala

Mitchell, Stephen (2011): Witchraft and Magic in the Nordic Middle Ages. University of Pensylvania Press

Mortensson-Egnund, Ivar (1993): Edda-Kvede Det Norske Samlaget, Oslo

Rygh, Karl (1871): Norske og islandske tilnavne frå oldtiden og middelalderen - Trondhjem

Simek, Rudolf (1996): Dictionary of Northern Mythology Translated by Angela Hall, D.S. Brewer, Cambridge

Solli, Brit (2002): SEID Myter, sjamanisme og kjønn i vikingenes tid Pax Forlag A/S, Oslo

Steinsland, Gro/Meulengracht Sørensen, Preben (1999):Voluspå Pax forlag A/S, Oslo

Strömbäck, Dag (2000): SEJD och andra studier i nordisk själsuppfatning Kungl. Gustav Adolfs Akademien för svensk folkkultur, Gidlunds förlag, Uppsala

Turner, Victor W (1996): Betwixt and Between – the liminal period in rites de passage (in Eriksen, ed., 1996)
Van Gennep, Arnold (1999): Overgangsriter = Rites de Passage Oversatt av Erik Ringen, Pax Labyrint, Oslo

ENDNOTES

1 Kvilhaug, Maria (2012): The Seed of Yggdrasill – Deciphering the Hidden Messages of Old Norse Myths, Whyte Tracks, Denmark

2 Steinsland, Gro/Meulengracht Sørensen, Preben (1999): Voluspå, Pax forlag, Oslo

3 Heimdallr = "Great World" from ON heimr = "world" and dallr = "splendid", "awesome", "great", "dazzling". An Aesir/Vanir deity. Val-Father (Valfǫðr)= A heiti (nickname) for Óðinn. The val refers to those who died because they were chosen by the valkyriur, Freyia or Óðinn himself to come to Valhalla (Valhǫll – the Hall of the Chosen Dead) where these chosen dead would eventually become warriors to fight alongside the gods during Ragnarök. The popular notion that every warrior who died in battle would go to Valhalla and that this was the only criteria is challenged by the Edda heroic poetry, where the path to Valhalla goes through a mystic initiation (Kvilhaug, Maria: "The Maiden with the Mead", 2004). The word valr generally refers to the fallen in battle, and to the battle-field itself, and is also used as a heiti for "falcon" or "horse", animals associated with other-world journeys. It is strikingly similar to the word val (n) for "choice" or "chosen", but has a different etymology. The poets likely played on this similarity, as the concept of the valr being val (chosen) is a strong theme in mythology.

4 Iviði = "Witches Within Wood": Feminine plural of the feminine singular iviðia which was used to refer to a sorceress, witch or giantess, but which literally means "within wood", from i = "in" and viðr = "wood", "tree", "forest". Nine iviði are also mentioned as Heimdall´s mothers in the Edda poem Hyndlulióð, and in the Hrafnagaldr Óðins an iviðia is said to "bring forth the ages". The "mothers" of the present world appear to be identified as worlds in their own right. Miotuið – an old spelling of the joined words Miǫðr-viðr = "Mead Tree" (or "wood", "forest", as above). A metaphor for Yggdrasill, the world-tree.

5 Ar var alda = "In the beginning was the Wave" is a very controversial interpretation that is not found in other translations. My interpretation is based in the understanding that ár is the ON adverb ár which means "in the beginning". It follows that var ("was") refers to the singular noun which was in the beginning, namely alda, which, when a singular noun, means "wave" (feminine singular). Traditionally, the sentence is taken to mean "early in the old times" or "early in the beginning", understanding alda as a form of alðr, meaning "age".

My interpretation is, however, literal, grammatically correct and entirely probable. The sentence is also found in another Edda poem, Helgakvíða Hundingsbani hin fyrri, stanza 1, where the birth of Helgi is likened to the birth of the present universe:

Ár var Alda	In the beginning was the Wave
þat er arar gvllo,	when the eagles shrieked and
hnigo heilog votnaf himinfiol-	sacred water poured down
lom;	the mountains of heaven;
þa hafþi Helga	Then was the Sacred One
inn hvgom stora reyia said:	of powerful intent
Borghildr borit	born to Fortress Battle
i Bralvndi.	In the Grove of Bright Shine

Ymir = from ON ýmr = "sound", "murmur". A likeness to the Old Indian universal sound **aum**? According to Snorri Ymir was an inter-sexed giant who became the body of the world.

Gap var Ginnunga = "The Open Mouth of the Sacred Descendants was (existed)". From gap = "open mouth" (indicating something ready to swallow something), var = "was", "existed», ginnr = "sacred" and unga = genitive plural of ungr = "descendant", "child", "lineage"

6 Burs synir = "The Sons of Storage Chamber". According to Snorri, the first Aesir gods, Óðinn, Víli and Vé were the sons of Borr, son of Bur ("Storage Chamber"). They shaped the world ("lifted up the lands"?) out of the body of Ymir (see stanza 3).

•Sól = "Sun" - is described as a female character in the poem. Snorri named her among the ásyniur– the goddesses. The "halls" she own are the places of Earth and the planets.

•Jorðr – Earth – another ásynia – Aesir goddess, mother of all people, daughter of Nott (Night) and Óðinn, mother to Thór and to all lineages of life, receiver of the dead.

7 Máni = Moon, counted among the Aesir gods yet in known myths mainly known for his mysterious "power" (megin) and for being brother to the Sun goddess, hunted across the heavens as she is, for all eternity.
• Himinjodyr = "Door of the Steeds of Heaven". I suspect the Steeds of Heaven represent the planets. The Sun goddess somehow controls their mysterious "door".

8 Rǫkstól = "Chair of Fate" = Parliament Seat. The parliament (þing) of the "powers" (all the powers that rule the universe, including the Aesir) is held in the heart of the realm of the nornir – the goddesses of fate – and under their supervision. Hence the seat of parliament is called a chair of fate. 8 Rǫkstól = "Chair of Fate" = Parliament Seat. The parliament (þing) of the "powers" (all the powers that rule the universe, including the Aesir) is held in the heart of the realm of the nornir – the goddesses of fate – and under their supervision. Hence the seat of parliament is called a chair of fate.

9 Iðavǫllr = "Field of Streams Returning to Watersource" – iða is genitive plural of iðr (feminine singular), a stream that separates from the main stream and returns to the source.

10 Gold is a known Old Norse metaphor for divine wisdom and knowledge.

11 The three all-mighty maidens from the Giant World are probably the norns, goddesses of fate, since fate is all-mighty, overruling even the gods. The word for "giant" – jötunn – originally meant "devourer".

12 Brímir= "Fire", Bláinn = "The Blue" – a poetical way of describing a rotting corpse, the dead

13 Móðsognir = "Shape-Searcher" is one possible interpretation of this name among several, which I have discussed in my book The Seed of Yggdrasill (2012), chapter II.9. The concept of something seeking out/searching for/drawing in an image, mark, stamp or shape appears the most probable and meaningful interpretation, especially seen in connection to the idea that the dwarfs are, or make, "images of men".

14 Names of primordial dwarfs.

15 Names of Dwarfs are listed. The vǫlva also addresses her main listener, the "Ruler" and "Counsel Wise"(Óðinn). Elves tend to represent souls of ancestors. Wind is a metaphor for death and mortality.

16 List of names of dwarfs continue.

17 The dwarfs of Hibernation/Law are introduced, they who were sent to the Earth Fields from the "Gravel Fields". Aurvangir could also be translated "Out of Falseness" or "Gravel Falseness" (illusion?)

18 Among these special dwarfs are also Óðinn (The High One). This corresponds with how the Aesir come out of the flock of dwarfs – namely the dwarfs of Laws and Hibernation who came to Earth in stanza 14. The arrival of the Three gods correspond poetically with the Three fate-maidens who arrived in stanza 8.

19 The "dwarfs of the Laws" are further listed.

20 Askr= "Ash" – the first man. All male trees symbolize men. Embla – uncertain meaning, possibly "linden" – all female trees symbolize women. Snorri Sturlusson claimed that the first man and woman were driftwood on the shore found by the Aesir Óðinn, Hænir and Hlóðurr, who by their gifts (see next stanzas) gave them life and humanity. The Aesir derive from the special dwarfs that they created on a previous level, as if to say the spiritual entities came to Earth through the physical shapes or images of the "man-image"-dwarfs.

21 The gifts of the Aesir are bestowed on humankind, equally on men and women: breath, spirit, poetry, mind, vitality and vivid, beautiful colors. The three Aesir are likely Óðinn, Víli and Vé, although the two latter ones are given descriptive nicknames. Víli – "Will", "Intent", corresponds with The Heat, whereas Vé – "Awe", "Sacred Space" – corresponds with "Chicken" – the giver of thought.

The name "Chicken" (in plural) is funny and mysterious on a character that actually bestows intelligence to human kind – perhaps the incessant clucking of chicken is a metaphor for how the thinking mind makes noise?

22 The World Tree Yggdrasill (Old Steed) is introduced, as is the well it grows from. The bright shining gravel is, according to Snorri, poured over the roots of the tree in order to rejuvenate it and counteract the steady decay of the tree. The tree represents the present universe. A tree is also a metaphor for a human being. The World Tree corresponds with the first man, Askr, since they are both called "Ash". The universe is often described as if it was a very large human being or human-like entity or a god. Heimdallr – "The Great World"– is likely another way of describing the conscious, divine universe.

The Well from which the gravel is poured has the quality of resurrecting and rejuvenating and transforming whatever and whoever submerges in it. In fact, Snorri claimed that those who bathed in the Well of Origin would emerge shining, bright and transparent like the membrane on the inside of the egg-shell.

The Well of Origin lies in the heart of divine realm Ásgarðr, is owned by the oldest norn, Urðr ("Origin"), and is where the parliament of the gods ("Chairs of Fate") takes place everyday – where the rulers of the universe meet to discuss all kinds of matters.

23 The norns – goddesses of fate – are introduced. The three original norns represent past, present and future. They are the most powerful beings in the universe and are probably identical to the three almighty giantesses that ordered the creation of the dwarfs in stanza 8.

This stanza indicates how fate operates, where the future is the accumulated "debt" of past and present working together - carving runes (symbols, rules, decisions) into the wood (matter) of the tree (universe).

To "carve in wood" meant to make runes. Thus the runes are also introduced for the first time, obviously related to fate and the powers of fate/time. The fact that the future is a result of how past and present "carve" together into the universal matter indicates how fate (the future) could be changed by those who practiced the art of divinatory seiðr – by controlling the present "carving" and thus altering the outcome, changing what is due – the debt that the future owes.

The norns emerge from the Well of Origin, just as the World Tree does. We could regard the Well of Origin as the liquid womb that birthed the present universe. The male tree and the female fate emerge together from this cosmic source.

According to Snorri Sturlusson in the Prose Edda, all individuals are followed throughout their lives by norns who emerge from the Well of Origin at their birth.

There are three kinds of norns – divine, elfin and dwarfish. Those who have a dwarfish norn get small and insignificant fates. The dwarfish norns are "the daughters of Dvalinn" – the daughters of Hibernation, indicating that they are sleepwalking and thus spinning insignificant and random fates for their individual. Myths about waking up ones norn abound, suggesting that once awakened, the norn will be divine or elfin.

24 Gullveigr = "Gold Power Drink" – from ON gull = "gold", "golden", and veigr = "strength", "power", "drink" (strong drink, alcoholic drink), sometimes used to describe the precious mead. In my thesis (2004) and book (2012) I offer an analysis of the burning of Gullveigr in the context of an initiation ritual, seeing as the next stanza shows the resurrected lady operating as a professional witch performing seiðr.
The witch is a disguise for Freyia, the goddess of the Vanir, who subsequently are attacked by Óðinn and the Aesir. Freyia, like the Vǫluspá vǫlva, is the first to introduce the art of seiðr - how to divine and change fate. The reference to a power drink indicates the "precious mead" that is frequently served by a female entity of the Underworld to gods and heroes who undergo initiation.

25 Gullveigr/Freyia is now called Heiðr – which means "bright", "illuminated", or more specifically a "bright open space", also giving name to English "heath" and "heathen". The taking of a new name is common after initiation. After her trial of fire, where the witch-goddess demonstrated her immortality through eternal resurrection, she travels the world like a vǫlva performing seiðr. Later, when the Vanir are incorporated into the pantheon of the Aesir, she teaches them the art of seiðr (according to Ynglinga saga 4, Snorri Sturluson).

26 The divine parliament discusses what happened to Gullveigr (the loss) and who is to pay for it. What exactly is the loss is uncertain. Many have suggested that the problem is the burning itself, since the Vanir would likely demand compensation for the torturing of their kinswoman, but as mentioned earlier, the trial by fire may have been an initiation where the goddess displayed how to conquer death.
I suspect that the loss has to do with the fact that the goddess now walks the world of men and giants in the shape of a witch - and is thus lost to the divine realm. The goddess has left the divine sphere, is wandering the world and teaches the art of seiðr to human women. She is creating the institution of witches to the benefit of people, yet she is lost to the divine realm and to the gods who need her.

There is a possible connection to Snorri´s story of how Freyia walked the world searching for her lost husband Óðr (Óðinn). Everywhere she went she took upon herself new shapes and new names, and left tears of red gold (wisdom, knowledge) behind.

27 The entry of the divine witch Freyia in the human world – and the burning, persecution or initiation ritual that preceded it was the cause of a parliament where the Aesir faced the burden of "the loss" (of the goddess?) alone. Óðinn mysteriously reacted to this threat by waging war against the Vanir, who are then victorious. From Snorri, we know that the Aesir managed to turn their own loss to their own favor by cunningly devising a truce that allowed them to welcome the Vanir into their fold. Thus Freyia could teach the Aesir the art of seiðr.

28 Poetry´s Maiden (Óðs mey) is Freyia, but could also be Iðunn, who was married to the god of poetry. Both goddesses, who are proba-bly one and the same, were abducted by giants or threatened to be so. The story probably also refers to a myth rendered below (footnote 26).
Jotunn (m.sg.) is usually translated as "giant". Here, I offer the literal translation, which is "devourer" – a power of consuming destruction.

29 The thunder-god takes action at parliament, waging war and breaking oaths. The only reference that may explain this stanza is the story told by Snorri of how a giant was engaged to build a protective wall around the divine realm, being promised Freyia, Sun and Moon as a reward if he could manage this within a certain time. When the Aesir realize that the giant might succeed, they must make the only deity not present when the oath was made, Þórr, do the dirty work of breaking their promises.

30 "She" is the vǫlva, either Freyia/Gullveigr/Heiðr or the ancient vǫlva who divines this poem - or both – there might not be a difference between the two. The older witch could be an older aspect, referring to herself as "I" in the present and as "she" in the past, when she was younger. The listening attention of the Great World is somehow lost to the world, a tragedy connected to Óðin´s lost (wagered) eye. According to Snorri, Óðinn sacrificed his one eye to the Well of Memory in order to get a drink of the precious mead of Memory where all the accumu-lated knowledge of the universe is stored. The radiant tree is the world tree, the universe.

31 The encounter between Óðinn and the witch who divines this poem and/or was burned in his hall earlier (Freyia) is now described – the prelude to the very divination of the Vǫluspá. The encounter appears laden with past conflicts, it is as if the witch-goddess is telling the old god "what did I say?" She refers once more to the wager of Óðin´s eye into the Well of Memory as a crucial event - perhaps it is what has caused the destruction to come?

32 Óðinn (The Father of Armies) now acts like any Viking Age person who seeks the counsel of a vǫlva: He offers gifts so that she will give wise counsel and prophecy the future. Although placed in the middle of the poem, the story presented here is the prelude to stanza 1, where the witch addresses a universal audience at the bequest of Óðinn. The bequest happened here, just after the first war in the world, where the All- Father worries about the future course and needs to understand its origin.

33 The arrival of the valkyriur – the Fates/Norns of warriors – heralds an age of war.

Among the valkyriur mentioned are Skuld ("Debt"), the norn (fate) of the future, and Gǫndul ("The Magician"), which is a name for Freyia in a myth where the goddess is forced to arrange a conflict leading to perpetual war between two former friends, the prince of the Danes and the prince of the Arabs, so that she may retrieve her stolen necklace (source: Flateyiarbók).

34 The vǫlva speaks of herself in the first person as she describes how she divined the fate of Óðin´s and Friggs son, Baldr ("The Courageous One"), thus identifying herself as the dead witch that lies to the east of the gates of Hel´s halls in the Edda poem Vegtamskviða, the witch who first divined Baldr´s death.

Mistletoe: Frigg had demanded of all things on Earth that they do not harm Baldr, but the mistletoe, being "too young" (or else the one earthly being that never touches the Earth) had not received the message.

35 The mistletoe was used by Loki to make an arrow that, shot by the blind Hǫðr ("Strife"), killed Baldr.

Óðinn immediately went about begetting a "son" called Váli ("The Choice"), which could kill Strife the Blind.

36 Váli, the son of Odin, is said to immediately go about his business of avenging Baldr as soon as he is born. Understanding that Váli means "Choice" makes it possible to understand the impossible – how a newly born babe can begin fighting. It is not a baby at all but a choice made: the choice to "kill" or bring to the "pyre" that which Baldrs killer represents: "Strife the Blind". Frigg, knowing all fate, weeps in her abode Fensalar "The Moist Halls".

37 Another, conflicting Choice is also presented: Loki´s "son", also called Váli ("The Choice"), which causes the twisting of the "warbonds" within the entrails (the metaphorical "guts") of people. These twisted entrails keep Loki captive, as we see in the next stanza.

38 Loki is bound by the entrails of his own Choice within the "Grove of Cauldrons" (Hveralundr) – his Choice to kill what Baldr represents: Courage and a wide view of the world (his abode is called Breidablik –
The Broad Vision. Sigyn ("Victory Woman") is his wife, who protects him against the poison dripping down in his face, but can only do so temporarily. As soon as the cup she holds beneath the stream of poison is full, it has to be emptied, and Loki writhes in agony.

39 The river of Hel (the border between life and death) is introduced, here by the name "Sharp One". This river shows up with many different names in the myths. This name indicates death by sharp weapons.

40 Niðavellir = from niðar which indicates the waning moon or the time of no moon. Nið could otherwise indicate shame and humiliation. Here lies the hall of Sindri (Glowing Spark), the master smith dwarf who forged the golden bear Gullinborsti, the magical golden ring Draupnir (which drips eight new rings like itself every ninth night), and the lightning bolt hammer of the Thundergod.
The Never Cooling is probably another way to indicate Muspell, the cosmic sphere of intense heat and poisonous gases described by Snorri, which is ruled by Surtr (The Sooty One). Here, he is called Brimir, which means Fire, and is identified as a iotunn – which is usually translated as "giant" but which actually means "devourer".

41 The High Hall of Hel is described here in its most somber aspect. Serpents represent transformation (the shedding of skin), associated with what happens in death.

42 In the river that forms the border to Hel, between life and death, the unworthy must wade for eternities, slowly sucked dry by the great serpent Shame Biter (or Dark Moon Biter, Waning Biter, or simply Biter Below). The unworthy are oath-breakers, "murdering wolves", which indicates those who murder for the sake of their greed, and rapists (those who by force take the girlfriends of others). Women are here called eyra-runar – "ear-runes", rune meaning a secret, a fate, or a symbol. It indicates that women are thought of as the confidantes to their mens´ secrets.

43 The Old One is a female (from the grammatical form of "in aldna" whose identity would have been obvious to the Viking Age audience. To us, she is mysterious. But her abode in Iron Forest may indicate Skaði, who is said to live in Iron Forest, which is situated in Trymheimr, a part of the giant world. Like Skaði, the "Old One" is associated with wolves and the powers of death and destruction.

The Moon´s abductor is mentioned by Snorri as a giant in wolf-disguise who perpetually hunts the Moon, forcing it to perpetually flee across the heavens. One day, the wolf is fated to eat the Moon, just like another is fated to eat the sun and a third to eat Óðinn.

44 "It" is likely the troll-wolf that will devour the Moon, which is associated and likely symbolizes the negative quality of Greed ("the kindred of Greed").

45 Fjalarr may mean "Deceiver" or "Spy" or "Hider" from the verb fela (to hide, spy, deceive). The meaning is uncertain, however. Fjalarr also appears in a story where he is one of the two mischievous dwarfs who want to monopolize knowledge. They did this by killing off the creature Kvasir, who represented omniscience, once walking freely available to everyone on earth – until Fjalarr and his friends killed him and stored his blood in cauldrons. The Gallows Wood probably refers to the place of initiation, since Óðinn was initiated by a hanging sacrifice ritual in order to retrieve the blood in the hidden cauldrons, which had become the mead of poetry.

46 Two more "roosters" herald the apocalypse; one in Valhǫll, another in Hel.

47 "Gluttony" (Garmr) is another representation of "Greed" (Fenrir, or the Fenris-wolf), who is destined to run loose and wreak havoc before and during Ragnarǫk ("The Fall of the Rulers"), which is the apocalypse divined to take place before the new Earth may be reborn. These lines are repeated several times in the poem to come. The wolf running free refers to how the Greed-Wolf was bound by the gods (by the god of war), who while binding Greed «lost an arm» to it. The witch refers to "she" who divined these things the first time – now she is older and knows even more.

48 A little description of social life before the apocalypse.

49 The last battle is heralded by the blowing of the Bellowing Horn by Heimdallr ("The Great World"), whereas Óðinn consults universal Memory.
50 The «sefi» - souls or "sleepers" are somehow swallowed up by the realm of Surtr (The Sooty One), Muspell, which is the realm of heat and poisonous gases.

51 As much as the physical world is destroyed, the fate of gods, the souls of the dead and the dwarfs (who give shape and form to life) is still at stake.

52 These lines repeat those of stanza 44

53 "Weakening" is the "giant" Hrymr, whose name may be related to the words hrymast (to weaken) or hrymdr, "weak" or "weakling" or hruma – "to make weak". This weakening comes from the symbolical "east" – the realm of the devourers (iotnir, otherwise often known as "giants"). Great Magic is Jǫrmungandr – the Middle World Serpent, who now twists, creating huge waves in the ocean. The shrieking eagle is likely Hræsvelgr – "Corpse Swallower" – a symbol of death being announced. The Nail Traveler is the ship that heralds the last battle between Aesir (gods of conscious and spiritual and vital powers) and the Iotnir (the devourers, giant powers that consume the world).

54 Muspell – the primeval cosmic realm of heat and poison gases. With them, from the East, comes Loki, steering the ship of death. He is here called the "brother of Byleistr". Byleistr/Byleiptr may be derived from the words bylr ("wind") and leiptr ("lightning").Wind is a metaphor for death.

55 Surtr ("The Sooted One"), the giant who rules in Muspell, the realm of heat and poisonous gases, attack from the south, which is also the direction from which the gods and the sun goddess originate. He wields the sword of the Sun goddess´ shine. When the rock wall or mountain wall falls, troll women seem to be either hurling matter or hurling themselves – it was thought that troll women dwelled beneath the earth and were the cause of volcanic activity and movement within the earth, especially moving rocks and mountains. Thus this could be an image of how the Earth´s crust breaks.

56 Frigg´s first sorrow was the death of her son Baldr. Her second sorrow is the death of her husband Óðinn. This stanza could appear to identify Óðinn and Freyr, as they are both described walking towards their nemesis for their final battle, and then described as one when they die: as Frigg´s pleasure.

Óðinn, representing Spirit, has to fight Greed, whereas Freyr, representing cultivated nature and fertility, must fight The Sooty One, who represents heat and poison (pollution?). They both die in the battle, but their last battle also leads to the deaths of the giant opponents.

When Freyr is called Slayer of the Bellower, the poet refers to a myth told by Snorri where Freyr fights the Bellower (Beli) and kills him with an antler (Freyr has given away his sword). The myth is obscure but seems to take place at Ragnarǫk, which may signify that the Bellower and the Sooty One are the same being.

57 This stanza repeats stanza 44 and 49 and was probably functioning as a refrain

58 Óðin´s son Viðarr, a name which could either be translated "Wood
(=Human) Warrior" or "Expander", known for his silence, and born by Truce (Griðr), avenges his father by killing the wolf of Greed once and for all. The wolf of Greed (Fenrir) is here known as the son of the Lineage of the Roarer (Hveðrung – which also could mean the lineage of the Ram, beasts of Thor).

59 Þórr, here known as the Protector of the Middle World and as the Son of Earth (Life Struggle), enters his final battle against the Middle World Serpent, whose twisting body causes the earth to shake and the oceans to rise. The thundergod walks "the nine steps", which is a metaphor for dying or for initiation. The god who is so often made fun of in poetry earns a lack of scorn – which is a typical understatement meaning that he will be praised for his valiant death.

60 The Sun goddess and the Earth goddess appear to succumb to the disaster as the Sun is blackened and the Earth flooded.

61 Another repetition of the refrain.

62 The Earth is reborn more beautiful than ever. From another poem, we know that the Sun is also reborn, or rather bears a daughter that will walk in her mother´s ancient paths.

63 The Iðavellir – Plains of the Streams Returning to Source, from the word iðr, which means a small stream that separates from the main stream and returns to the water source. It is also the word that makes the name Iðunn – the goddess of resurrection and rejuvenation – transformation and renewal, and thus immortality.

The Earth Girdler is the Middle World Serpent, being discussed at parliament by the resurrected gods, the events are remembered, as is the secrets (runes) of Óðinn (the Great Sage).

64 Before fate entered the cosmic scene, the gods had been playing with "golden chequers" and had no care in the world. These are no found again, surfacing in the grass of the new earth.

65 Baldr returns from the Underworld, representing Courage ("baldr") and a broad vision ("Breidablik"), as in greatness and open-ness of mind. The Shattered One is Óðinn and his battlefield is life. Strife (Hǫðr) is reconciled with his brother, probably meaning that the quality of struggle and battle exists in harmony with courage and wisdom.

66 "Chicken" – Hænir – the god that gave mind, poetry and thinking to humankind, chooses rune staves for divination, indicating that intel-ligence is applied in order to divine the future.

The Wide World of Winds is the universe moved by the unseen winds of the cosmic source – winds associated with death. Thus it is the mortal world we are speaking of, where peaceful coexistence now rules.

67 Gim-lé = "Shielded from Fire" – a realm of immortality where the resurrected gods now dwell?

68 The arrival of the one who rules everyone is often thought of as a Christian concept - either the poet was influenced by the Christian concept of the return of Christ, or was trying to show how Christ would arrive. The one who is more powerful than everything is also mentioned in the poem Hyndlulióð, stanza 44. That poem, however, also seem to indicate that the one that came before and unites everything is Heimdallr, "The Great World" – and thus the living universe. It is possible that this is a part of a pantheist idea of universal oneness.

69 The Shame Biter/The Waning Biter makes his last appearance – or else his first in the new world – the one who consumes the dead in Hel. The wish to sink may be explained by identifying the witch of the Vǫluspá with the witch of the Vegtamskviða, where the diviner is a dead witch made to rise from her grave.

70 Óðinn = Yggr = The Terrible One/The Old One. Battle-Dust´s father=The Powerful Head Veil

71 Interestingly, the word for «welcome» here is «andföngr», literally translating as "spirit-embrace/catch"

72 A river is, by definition, always female in Old Norse language and myth. This particular river is "Impetuosity", but could also mean "Violence" (in a rash, impulsive angry-laden form)

73 The Sooted One (Surtr) is destined to lead the army against the gods during Ragnarök (see the Völuspá)

74 "Slight Death" is an interpretation based on the name Narfi, meaning either "narrow" or "corpse", a character identified with Nárr/Nörr, meaning "narrow, slight".

75 From this verse derives the Old Norse poetical metaphors where wind or breeze is used to describe death (or impending death), and also the use of "wind-shielded" or "breeze-less" to describe immortality.
76 God of "winds" and "waves" (invisible movements and vibrations of the cosmos)

77 Hamingjur are goddesses/spirits closely attached to humans, perhaps their souls, or fates, thought to be fortune-bringing aspects of the norns, possibly the part of the soul which can travel outside of the body, shape-shifting qualities (see The Seed of Yggdrasill for more analysis)

78 The verse is describing prophesied events AFTER the apocalypse and the new and better world to come

79 The verse refers to a mysterious and unexplained event otherwise described by Snorri Sturlusson in his Prose Edda, the Gylfaginning, where Odin approaches his dead son on the pyre: "Then was the body of Baldr borne out on shipboard...Odin laid on the pyre that gold ring which is called Draupnir; this quality attended it, that every ninth night there dropped from it eight gold rings of equal weight. Baldr's horse was led to the bale-fire with all his trappings..."

Later, the myth continues by describing how Frigg asks who among the gods is willing to travel into Hel in order to attempt to resurrect Baldr. The one who volunteers is Hermódr, who borrows Odin´s eight-legged steed Sleipnir: "Now this is to be told concerning Hermódr, that he rode nine nights through dark dales and deep, so that he saw not before he was come to the river Gjöll and rode onto the Gjöll-Bridge; which bridge is thatched with glittering gold..."

In Hel, Hermódr is well received by Baldr and his wife Nanna, who keep a great banquet in the hall of Hel, and if Baldr may not be re-stored, so Odin gets the ring Draupnir back from the world of the dead: "Then Hermódr arose; but Baldr led him out of the hall, and took the ring Draupnir and sent it to Odin for a remembrance. And Nanna sent Frigg a linen smock, and yet more gifts, and to Fulla a golden fin-ger-ring."

80 Veratýr – "God of Being" = Odin

81 Ullr was an ancient pre-Viking Age god of hunting and archery, associated with Freyr [god of growth, crops, royalty, civilization, culti-vated nature and masculine sexuality]. Elves are associated with souls.

82 Saga=History=Frigg

83 Hroptr=Shattered One=Odin

84 Thiazi=Slave-Binder, the eagle of Death, creating all the cosmic winds. See Vafþrúðnismál stanza

85 Harm=Skadi, goddess/giantess of death, injury, daughter to the Slave-Binder eagle

86 Heimdallr = "Great World", a divine personification of the living, conscious universe, all-seeing, all-hearing and all-remembering. One of several metaphors for the living body of Cosmos.

87 This is a way of saying that the goddess Freyia as head norn/ valkyria rules the fates of people

88 Vidarr=Wood Warrior or Expanding Warrior is a son of Odin with a giantess called "Truce" – he is silent, but he is also the one who will overcome the wolf of Greed after Odin has been devoured by it. Silent expansion of the human spirit.

89 Eldrhrimnir – "Fire Burner" is the name of the "boar" that is given to the Einherjar (Sole-Rulers, those who can rule themselves) in Valhalla. The verse clearly points out that this boar, as well as the cook and the cauldron, are secret riddle-words for whatever metaphysical/ alchemic substance that the immortal/endlessly resurrecting warriors are nourished by.

90 Geri and Freki are Odin´s "wolves", representing action and de- sire/greed, controlled by Spirit

91 People-Witness (or Great Witness), Thióðvitni, is one of the names for the great "wolf" of greed and gluttony. The word for "people" refers to unspecified tribes/nations and originally meant "many" or "great"

92 The river is the boundary between the worlds of the living and the dead, the realm of the divine immortals such as Valhalla and the realms of oblivion in death. Those who rejoice in slaughter may not cross so easily. See Vǫluspá stanza 39, where murderers, oath-breakers and rapists are doomed to wade in the river Cutting

93 Bílskírnir = Diminishing Shine is the hall of Thor (Thunder), Odin´s son and protector of Mother Earth. The hall lies in the "Power Fields" (Thrudvangar) where the god of thunder and lightning resides, protecting the Earth against assaults from rock giants from Utgard (Outer World) – an archaic description of the atmosphere (the "roof")?

94 The "she-goat" is the goddess producing the mead of resurrection that grants gods, elves and immortal human beings their renewed im- mortality, the "mead" in Valhalla

95 Hvergelmir, the Resounding Mill, is the well of Hel (Death) where one of the roots to the world tree is situated, to where all souls go after death to be ground into nothing, and from where all the "rivers" of the world originate

96 The ash Yggdrasill is a metaphor for the universe

97 These are Valkyriur, the Fates (norns) of war and warriors

98 The steeds that are pulling the chariot of the Sun – the verse explains why they (or we) are not over- heated, due to some mysterious cooling device made by the gods from iron.

99 The Sun is a goddess in Norse lore, but is sometimes referred to by the more gender-neutral "deity"

100 The "bright bride of Heaven" and the "shine-skinned deity" refer to the Sun goddess

101 Freyr represents cultivated nature and civilization and fertility, a child of the "wind and waves". Wood is a metaphor for matter, life and the physical human being, hence his ship, "Woodchips", is made of this.

102 Odin´s eight-legged steed able to take him into all the different cosmic worlds

103 "Sons of victorious gods" refer to human beings

104 The benches and drinking banquet of Aegir, the god of the ocean and father to all the world´s "waves" and "rivers" (his daughters), and thus identifiable with Njörd, is a metaphor for the final destination of the immortal gods, elves and enlightened human beings, as described in Snorri´s Skaldskaparmál (see my work "The Seed of Yggdrasill" for more in-depth analysis.
105 Odin

106 Having the goddesses (the disir) against you is a metaphor for being doomed to die
107 *Skaði´s eagle-giant father, a symbol of devouring death and oblivion

108 *"She" ("hennar") refers to Grotti – the Mill of Fate from within the Earth
109 *Leikur can mean "plays" and "sports" but also means "lovers", "playmates", and "girlfriends" – but it is not said who they are "play-mates" with...

110 Aurr- Mud-Sand is also the word used to describe the element that the oldest norn Urðr uses to revive the world tree Yggdrasill every day.

111 "Illusion – Silegia – literally: "Eye-Filter"

112 Death

113 Óðinn

114 Hermóðr is the hero who, like a shaman, tried to rescue the dead Baldr from Hel. On this occasion he was given the horse Sleipnir and other equipment from Óðinn.

115 Sigmundr Völsung

116 «Within-Matter» is my interpretation of the metaphorical meaning of the name «Innsteinn», literally translating as «In-Stone». As I have explained in The Seed of Yggdrasill, rock matter may be a metaphor for matter, the material. The stone is also a metaphor for death (burials), for those who dwell within the mounds, ancestors.

117 Gold in these myths is a metaphor for divine wisdom, in this case the wisdom belonging to the mysterious "chosen dead", those who have died and been resurrected as immortal souls who dwell in service to the gods against the powers of destruction.

118 Alf = «Elf» = Soul. Wolf = greed, desire, action. The «sea» could be the cosmic ocean (star heaven). Swan is an animal often used as a metaphor for fate (the norns appear in swan shape), the red color is associated with blood and mortality.

119 Hlédís – from hlé = wind-shielded place, shelter from the wind. Wind is a metaphor for death, wind- shield or breezeless are metaphors for immortality. Dis means "goddess", Gydja means "priestess". She is the goddess of resurrection and immortality, a result of Wisdom and Love together.

120 Váli/Ali=»Choice» or «Chosen» - he «chose» to destroy the Blind Strife that killed Baldr (symbol of the great mind, living in «Broad View»).

121 Battle-Combat is the Mother to Elm-Power-Drink, who is the ancestral mother to all the world´s lineages (see st.15-16). The elm is a metaphor for "woman" (as are all female trees, as well as for goddess or any other female character), the power-drink refers to the drink of resurrection and immortality.

122 Svafa=Sleeper (feminine), also possibly meaning «soul» - otherwise known as a valkyria who keeps reincarnating to meet her reborn lover (the Sea-King) in the Edda heroic poetry.

123 Thora is the female form of Thor (Thunder, also representing thought and mind). Day is the day, possibly as in enlightenment, a new beginning.
    Furious Ocean is a giant/devourer representing fury and emotion. Girdle may refer to the Middle Earth Serpent that girdles the world and forms a boundary between the lands of gods, men and giants.
    The two Greeds (Frekis) are the "wolves" that threaten Sun, Moon and life itself.

124 The Kettle refers to what may contain the mead of poetry, inspiration, wisdom and immortality

125 Wind is a metaphor for death/mortality

126 Nanna is Baldr´s wife, who stays with him in Hel. The meaning of her name is uncertain, it has been speculated that she is a borrowing from the ancient Sumerian goddess Inanna, who also followed the young, bright god who was her lover into the underworld and stayed part-time there. If her name is Old Norse in origin, it may be from the word nönna = "woman" (later the origin of the word "nun"). Like Síf, whose name just means "female relative", her name may simply signify that she is the female counterpart to Baldr – or his fate/soul (female characters in Norse myths often represent the inner soul or fate of their kinsmen).

127 Linen is a metaphor for «fate». The two "brothers" are also mentioned in stanza 25 (next page)

128 A giant in eagle-disguise is a common Old Norse metaphor for the cosmic power of death, such as Thiazi (Slave-Binder) and Hræsvelgr (Corpse-Swallower) who creates the unseen «winds» that stir all the worlds
129 The famous wolf is likely a reference to the Greed-wolf

130 I chose not to leave this name as it is because it is a direct reference to the particular Sigurd Völsung who in Edda heroic poetry, during a rite of initiation, slayed the serpent Fafnir and who because of this and his great wisdom achieved divine immortality in the arms of his valkyria. He represents initiation, enlightenment, and resurrection/immortality.

131 Fafnir means The Embracer, a symbol of the Middle Earth Serpent who separated the worlds between gods and men. When he is slain, Sigurd achieves the divine wisdom needed to wake up his valkyria-fate (his divine fate, one of resurrection and enlightenment). The Masked One is Odin.

132 Völsungar – from völ=wand, magic staff, the sort carried by the vǫlur (witches, oracles)

133 Giuki is the legendary ancestor of the Niflungar in Edda heroic poetry, meaning of this name is unknown. His children, Gunnarr (Battle-Warrior), Högnir (The Thinker) and Gudrun (Divine Symbol) are close to Sigurd. Their characters are loosely based on historical people such as Gundahar of the Burgunds, but as they appear in the Edda their roles are metaphorical and important to the story of the crooked path towards enlightenment. Gudthorm, "Divine Mercy", is the one who is tricked into killing Sigurd.

134 The characters mentioned in this verse are known legendary and probably historical characters; Ivarr was the last Skioldunga king from Scania, who overthrew the Ynglingar and became the first king to unite all the Swedish tribes and besides became king of Denmark. No king before him had ruled so many tribes as one nation. His daughter, Aud the Deep-Minded, was the female end of the Skioldunga lineage. With Hrærek (Rurik, Roderick, Rodrigo), known as the "Ring-Slinger" (meaning that he was generous with wealth), she had the famed king Harald Wartooth who died ca. 750 AD.

His father, Hrærek, threatened to deny the throne of Denmark-Sweden to Harald, so Aud the Deep-Minded sought alliance with Rárbard, a sea-king (meaning a Viking who ruled great fleets but no land), with whom she had Randver, the father of Sigurd Ring, who came to rule Denmark, who maintained the peace with Charlemagne, and who was a father to Ragnar Lodbrok.

135 The Choice brought the killer of Baldr (broad view, objectivity, fairness) to the pyre. The killer was Hödr Blindi, "Blind Strife"

136 Aurr=sand, gravel, rock, stone, mud – the oldest norn, Urdr –"Origin", pours «aurr» onto the roots of the world tree Yggdrasill to rejuvenate it every day. Thus Aurbóda could be another name for her.

137 «Injury» is the literal translation of the name Skadi, otherwise known as a goddess of skiing and archery, but certainly a creature of death. Her father Thiazi (Slave-Binder) is fond of "shooting" (that is, of killing), being the eagle of Death.

138 A reference to the goat who produces the mead of immortality

139 Horse-thief – the horse is in Edda poetry a symbol of the steed,- vehicle which carries a soul onto the path of initiation or to visit between the worlds

140 Wood-Desire is an interpretation of the name Vídolfr. The latter part, olfr, means "wolf" and symbolizes desire, greed, survival-instinct, action (what keeps us alive). Wood is a metaphor for living matter, the material universe itself is "wood", people and gods are also made of "wood", so wood is a metaphor for flesh, the body, the material world.

141 "Magic-Wombs" refer to what we today may perceive as a male to female transsexual sorcerer, a male sorcerer with a womb for seid-birthing. Svarthofdi means "Black Head" but "head", just like "helmet", is a metaphor for mind, and black is a metaphor for darkness.

142 This is a reference to Heimdallr («Great World»), the divine personification of the universe, and the
Heimdalargaldr quoted by Snorri: "Of nine mothers am I child, of nine sisters am I son."

143 This stanza refers to Loki´s children: The Fenrir-Wolf (Greed), the Middle-World-Serpent (boundary between the worlds), Hel (Death). He had these three "children" by Angrbóda (Bids Anger). In a myth where Loki transforms into a mare in heath, (s)he is impregnated by the giant stallion Svadilfari (Misfortune-Traveler) and gives birth to Sleipnir, the eight-legged horse, "Glider", who can move between the worlds regardless of their boundaries, even into death. The "Brother of Byleistr (Lightning Storm) is Loki or Odin.

144 Linden, a feminine tree, is a metaphor for «woman» (or any other female being, such as a goddess). It is possible that this stanza refers to the woman who in Völuspá is burnt three times, and reborn three times.

145 Heimdallr, the Great World, a unifying original divine ancestor for absolutely all beings

146 Freyia is here likened to the she-goat Heidrún, Bright Open Space Symbol, who produces the mead of immortality in Valhalla. Hyndla, on the other hand, has nothing to give to the seeker of divine wisdom, being a representative of oblivion in death, even if she has revealed many secret tidings.

147 Unburnt – Freyia was, as we know, burnt and resurrected three times before she came among the immortal gods. Hyndla is the fate/death that leads to eternal sleep. The Witches Within Wood are the fate- spinners residing within the world (and within the nine previous worlds, as mentioned in the Völuspá).

148 Freyia and Hyndla reveal, in these last stanzas, how the two of them represent two different courses of fate (or perhaps of fate af- ter death) ; one of oblivion, destruction and apocalypse, the other of enlightenment and resurrection. Freyia is the one who may lead Ottarr (Fear-Warrior) to Valhalla (immortality, resurrection), and the giver of the precious drink of memory, poetry, inspiration and immortality. Hyndla may reveal all the hidden knowledge of the world, but in herself she desires but sleep, oblivion and total annihilation of the soul.

ABOUT THE AUTHOR

Maria Kvilhaug was born in Oslo, Norway, in 1975. She studied History of Religions and Old Norse Philology at the university of Oslo. She has written several non-fiction and fiction books concerning Old Norse pre-Christian culture and religion.

http://www.bladehoner.wordpress.com
http://www.youtubecom/user/ladyofthelabyrinth

NON-FICTION:
The Maiden with the Mead (2004/2009)
The Seed of Yggdrasill (2013/2018/2020)
The Poetic Edda, Six Cosmology Poem (2017/2021)
The Trickster and the Thunder god, Thor and Loki in Old Norse Myths (2018)

FICTION:
Blade Honer Series:
The Hammer of Greatness
My Enemy´s Head
The Hel-Rune´s Claim
A Twisted Mirror

The Three Little Sisters

The Three Little Sisters is an indie publisher that puts authors first. We specalize in the strange and unusual. From titles about pagan and heathen spirituality to traditional fiction we bring books to life.

https://the3littlesisters.com